ORBÁN VS. SOROS

ORBÁN
vs.
SOROS

···

THE FOUR-DECADE DUEL
• BETWEEN •
VIKTOR ORBÁN & GEORGE SOROS

GÁBOR G. FODOR
Translated by Michael Mansell
Edited by Rajmund Fekete

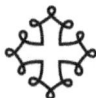

Angelico Press

The work on which the translation is based is G. Fodor
Gábor – *Orbán vs. Soros. Three chapters on the four-decade
struggle between Orbán and Soros*, Foundation for Research on
Central and Eastern European History and Society, 2024

The Angelico Press edition is published with the
support of the Foundation for Research on Central
and Eastern European History and Society.

ppr   979-8-89280-108-9
cloth   979-8-89280-110-2
ebook   979-8-89280-111-9

Book and cover design
by Michael Schrauzer

To George Soros

CONTENTS

ACKNOWLEDGMENTS
xi

INTERVIEWEES
xiii

PROLOGUE
1

2017
5

· I ·
The Unshaven Years
7

· II ·
A Hot Tin Roof
53

· III ·
The Duel
95

EPILOGUE
148

ACKNOWLEDGMENTS

THE WRITING OF *ORBÁN VS. SOROS* WAS preceded by in-depth research. I read everything I could about the two protagonists of our story, and talked to everyone I felt it might be worthwhile talking to. There were some who agreed, but who did not want their names made public; but now I can personally thank the others by name. For the valuable conversations I had with them, I thank the following, among others: Dorottya Baczoni, Zsolt Bayer, Márton Békés, János Betlen, Gábor Fodor, Péter Csermely, András Giró-Szász, János Gyurgyák, Gábor Horn, Zoltán Kovács, Collin McMahon, Zsolt Németh, Viktor Orbán, Bernadett Petri, József Szájer, Réka Szemerkényi, Attila Várhegyi, and Vilmos Velkovics. I thank the staff at the 21st Century Institute for our periodic meetings. My thanks are due to Rajmund Fekete and Márton Soltész for their conscientious editing, which was rapid and accurate—and, of course, to Michael Mansell for his irreplaceable work as the translator of this edition. I owe special thanks to Mária Schmidt for her ideas, her stories, her advice, and her insightful analyses. Without these, this book would not exist—or if it did, it would not be this book. Finally, but above all, I thank my wife, Zsófi, for her support, patience, and attention.

ACKNOWLEDGMENTS

INTERVIEWEES

DOROTTYA BACZONI, historian and expert on international relations, Director of the Institute of the Twentieth Century, editor of several books.

ZSOLT BAYER (1963−), Hungarian right-wing, conservative journalist and columnist, television personality, one of the founders of Fidesz, close associate of Hungarian prime minister Viktor Orbán.

MÁRTON BÉKÉS (1983−), historian, Research Director of the House of Terror Museum, Director of the Institute of the Twenty-first Century, author of books on the history of Fidesz and the Hungarian Right.

JÁNOS BETLEN (1946−), economist, interpreter, television personality, translator and secretary to George Soros in Hungary in the late 1980s.

PÉTER CSERMELY (1966−), right-wing journalist and columnist, television presenter, a leading figure in right-wing media.

GÁBOR FODOR (1962−), lawyer, liberal politician, founding member of Fidesz, leaving Fidesz in 1993 to join the Alliance of Free Democrats, Member of Parliament and government minister.

ANDRÁS GIRÓ-SZÁSZ (1970−), political scientist, historian, political adviser, government spokesman, State Secretary for Communications (2011–14), Senior Advisor to the Prime Minister on domestic policy.

JÁNOS GYURGYÁK (1956−), historian, sociologist, book publisher, newspaper editor, editor-in-chief of the periodical *Századvég* (1985–95).

GÁBOR HORN (1955−), liberal economist and politician, Member of Parliament (1994–2010), currently President of Republikon Institute, a confidant of George Soros in Hungary in the 1990s.

ZOLTÁN KOVÁCS (1969−), historian, politician, government spokesman, State Secretary for International Communications in the Orbán government, recipient of an MA from the George Soros-founded CEU.

COLLIN MCMAHON, (1968−), German-American writer, screenwriter who has written on Soros and Trump.

ZSOLT NÉMETH (1963–), economist, politician, founding member of Fidesz, Member of Parliament since 1990.

VIKTOR ORBÁN (1963–), Prime Minister of Hungary, President of Fidesz.

BERNADETT PETRI, lawyer, politician, expert on the EU.

MÁRIA SCHMIDT, historian, Director General of the House of Terror Museum, Chief Political Advisor to the Hungarian prime minister (1998–2002).

JÓZSEF SZÁJER (1961–), politician, founding member of Fidesz, Member of Parliament (1990–2004), Member of the European Parliament (2004–20), a key player in the drafting of the Fundamental Law of Hungary.

RÉKA SZEMERKÉNYI, economist, politician, Hungary's Ambassador to the United States of America (2015–17), former Senior Advisor to the Hungarian prime minister on Foreign Affairs and Security Policy.

ATTILA VÁRHEGYI (1963–), former party director of Fidesz.

VILMOS VELKOVICS (1970–), journalist, editor, television presenter.

PROLOGUE

THIS BOOK IS ABOUT TWO HUNGARIANS of outstanding talent. One is decades older than the other, yet they are contemporaries. Their paths have crossed several times. There were times when they seemed to be able to work together. The elder of them, George Soros, entered Hungarian politics in 1984 in midlife, extremely wealthy and energetic, full of plans for social change. He quickly struck a deal with the leaders of Hungary's one-party state, enabling him to launch the Soros Foundation, which has since become a household name around the world (I was among its first scholarship holders). The younger man, Viktor Orbán, burst onto the Hungarian political scene at the end of the 1980s, and immediately became the leader of the forces which brought down communism in Hungary, and the embodiment of the hope shared by those who wanted a new, democratic Hungary. Soros also quickly saw a future in him and funded a foreign study trip for him. It could have been the beginning of a beautiful friendship.

It was not to be. Because Orbán soon realized that what is free will cost the most. As a Member of Parliament and President of Fidesz, he stopped accepting Soros's support and refused his financial assistance, in order to preserve his freedom of action.

They never lost sight of each other, yet for years their paths did not cross again in a way that was publicly visible. But in 2015 it emerged that the future of Europe was at stake. In line with Hungarian national traditions, Orbán—defending his homeland, Hungarian identity, and Christianity— refused to allow Europe voluntarily to open its doors to new conquerors from other cultures, religions, and civilizations. He saw that behind this influx of migrants were Soros and his organizations. He decided to expose Soros's plan to resettle one million people.

So he declared war on Soros, who, by then, was one of the

most influential men in the world, with followers in European governments, in parliaments, in the thickets of American politics, in international organizations, and in the NGOs he had funded—which, by then, had spread around the world. Orbán put Soros's face on billboards in Budapest and all over Hungary. He made it clear to everyone who this man really was, what he was up to and what he was planning against Europe and Hungary. He lifted the veil on those controlled and funded by him: the army of politicians, NGOs and aid organizations, "objective, independent" experts and media figures serving him.

To do this, Orbán needed—and still needs—enormous courage, determination, and unshakable resolve. The war between him and Soros has been in progress ever since. Their duel has become a personal affair for both.

Soros and his organizations have cast their net all around the world, using the same methods to work for the same goals: the seizure of power. Meanwhile, Soros's opponents around the world watch Orbán with admiration, and urge him on as he takes it upon himself to defeat the dragon on their behalf. The duel between Orbán and Soros has now become the main front in world politics. On one side is Orbán, representing the sovereigntists, and on the other is Soros, embodying the globalist, homogenizing, imperial forces.

Soros is using every means possible to bring down Orbán and his followers. But now that Orbán has exposed not only Soros but also his methods, what he wants is clear to everyone. His name has become a byword for the external imposition of globalist, imperialist, repressive initiatives. He has become one of the world's most despised men. This struggle has made Orbán known, recognized, and popular worldwide, a global star. But the war continues.

Gábor G. Fodor's book is about this duel. In a concise and accessible way it sheds light on their respective goals as well as the causes and the divergent worldviews behind them. The struggle for our future—between a patriot and a citizen of the world.

Mária Schmidt

"*The best way to drive out the Devil, if he will not yield to texts of Scripture, is to jeer and flout him, for he cannot bear scorn.*"
Martin Luther

2017

THIS IS THE SECOND HOTTEST YEAR ON
Earth since global records began. In Hungary the summer
is hotter and slightly drier than in previous years. The
average temperature is almost two degrees above normal.
This is the year in which the singer of the worldwide hit
song "Lambada" is murdered in Brazil. In Hungary, "VV
Fanni," a former reality TV star, disappears, assumed to
have been murdered.

Europe is rocked by terror attacks, including at an Ariana
Grande concert at Manchester Arena, and in central areas
of London, Stockholm, and Barcelona.

And on the subject of shocks, at the beginning of the year
Donald Trump is inaugurated as the forty-fifth President
of the United States of America, and Brexit gets underway.
In July, Hungary is swamped by billboards: they show the
face of an old gentleman with the caption *"Don't Let Soros
Have the Last Laugh!"*

Everyone senses that this summer will be even hotter
than usual.

I

The Unshaven Years

1806

Legend has it that on the very day Napoleon defeated the Prussians and triumphantly led his troops into the city of Jena, the great German philosopher Hegel—oblivious to what was going on around him—was working on the final pages of his *magnum opus* (those confounded deadlines!). He only noticed the historic events around him when a stray bullet hit his window, sending shards of glass flying onto the table over which he was hunched as he arranged his manuscript. He went out on to his balcony just as Napoleon was passing by, leading his troops into the conquered city. Hegel's feet were almost rooted to the spot when he saw the world spirit, the world distilled into a single point: a figure on a horse, a human instrument at the service of divine purpose. The philosopher watched in rapture as the Emperor rode through his city.

What does this German philosopher, who grew up in an austere family environment, have to do with our story? Perhaps he provides an example that even the greatest among us can be mistaken.

Our culture is not unipolar. We cannot think of the world from a single perspective. There is, for example, the two-faced Janus, who was capable of both noble and ignoble deeds. In this he is like Western civilization itself: two brothers at odds with each other, mutually validating incompatibility, with good and evil embedded in the depths.

It is also a basic tenet of our culture that the question of good and evil is usually addressed by those on the side of good, because even in the troubled world we live in, we need the truth. But what is truth? If your truth is your truth and mine is mine, then we will be locked into our respective interpretations of good and evil, and our struggles for truth will never end. History will never arrive at any resolution.

So what if there is not one Hegelian world spirit, but two? Two contending world forces, each conditional on the other: two intellectual positions, two worldviews, two political positions. And as the embodiment of these, there are two people behind things; and in them — in their duel — the world in which we live is distilled.

And what if these two people — in whom, so to speak, the world spirit is embodied — happen to be Hungarian? Both are warriors. Both are fond of talking. Each tells his own story. And the world is always surprised at how honest Hungarians are when talking about their own thoughts.

All very well, but how do we know that they are the ones to listen to, and that what we see is the real deal? Well, because it is right here, right now! Or, as the historians will one day say: "right then."

....

According to Hegel, the great, imperceptible events in history mostly happen in silence (he may have been wrong about that too). But what is certain is that for a long time the opposition between the two heroes of our story is barely noticeable; and, in fact, it initially seems as if they were not opposed to each other, but rather united by common intentions and goals. Their encounters have also been rare and arbitrary, and always conducted in a civilized and cultured manner. In this there is no trace of irreconcilable conflict between them. Yet both embody opposing truths — even if this remains hidden as an invisible, barely perceptible, as yet unwritten political history. But because each in his own way represents an absolute, their clash is inevitable.

This book tells the story of the relationship over four decades between two outstandingly talented Hungarians, and their intersecting and mutually disruptive ambitions. It is the story of a boy from the village of Felcsút who rose from nothing (Orbán) and a Hungarian Jewish boy born in Budapest, who emigrated first to London, and then to America (Soros). One becomes Hungary's longest-serving prime minister; the other, a New York banker, perhaps the world's most powerful billionaire, and a statesman without a state. We are witnessing a duel: on one side is a masterly political leader, democratically elected on consecutive occasions and always by a large margin; and on the other side is an unelected speculator who is a constant threat to nation states, and another real *Numero Uno*. An unequal struggle, sometimes visible, sometimes not, between a Central European country defending its sovereignty and a global empire with an interest in creating chaos. At the end of the twentieth century and the dawn of the twenty-first, it is the story of a modern-day David and Goliath. Put another way, because they are both Hungarian, in the language of folktales: the story of the youngest prince and the seven-headed dragon, a story which will capture the human imagination for a long time to come.

1984

....

Éva met him at the airport—in what else but a Trabant 601 (the very name of the car is revealing: it means "companion, follower, sidekick")?* The man made for the car with a spring in his step, and threw himself into the front passenger seat. He had just arrived from America, and was keen to get to his accommodation. Éva got behind the wheel, but then suddenly leant down between his legs and started tinkering with something. The man could not understand what the young woman wanted. But all Éva wanted was to start the car. The only way to coax this little box made of Duroplast (a type of plastic) into motion was first to open a little fuel supply valve, which the ingenious East German engineers had located in the front passenger seat footwell. So you had to bend down there to open and close it. The man muttered to himself, "No way! How could anyone design a car like this?"

The man—George Soros—was griping about socialism's most commercially successful "people's car." He had no idea that in the US the beloved *Trabi*—as part of the socialist need for luxury and diversity—was also produced in limousine, deluxe, cabriolet, automatic transmission, and military jeep-style versions (the latter was the *Kübel,* and its civilian variant was the *Tramp*). Similarly, he could not have guessed that in just a few years the whole show would collapse, the Trabant would be discontinued, and this "little miracle" would become the most treasured possession of obsessive classic car collectors, a symbol of the overthrow of communism.

....

The year was 1984.

It was a year just like any other. People and things were in motion, but there was no significant change. Those in

---

* One of the most widely used and affordable cars in Eastern Europe during the Cold War, famed for the basic nature of its design and construction.

power were tyrannizing, and the opposition was opposing. There was peace and quiet, and the smell of excrement. In the Soviet Union, two general secretaries were buried within two years,* but the Red Star seemed to be "more lasting than bronze" (aere perennius). There was some agitation surrounding friendly countries' boycott of the Los Angeles Olympics, but the fact remains that Carl Lewis's four gold medals at those Olympics are still remembered by many—while who won, say, the pole vault at the socialist countries' substitute games in Kursk (the so-called "Friendship Games") could be a one-million-dollar quiz question. "Gina," by the Hungarian band Dolly Roll, was the top hit in the *Ifjúsági Magazin* ("Youth Magazine") charts (three of Dolly Roll's songs were in the top ten). Whether this means anything is anyone's guess. On the other hand, some people suspected that the publication of Arthur Koestler's novel *Darkness at Noon* by the samizdat publisher Szabad Idő ("Free Time") might have some significance. Also significant, perhaps, was the fact that Margaret Thatcher was the first British prime minister to visit Hungary, and that the Chancellor of West Germany, Helmut Kohl, went there; but the fact that the bloodthirsty Polish General Wojciech Jaruzelski was also visiting was a sign of inertia. There was stability and calm. In the midst of all this stability, one could still sense that the construction of socialism was tottering along. Major central price increases were announced several times during the year, while the National Bank of Hungary was borrowing ever more from the World Bank and the International Monetary Fund. Everyone knew it already, even if it was unspoken: we are in debt, we are flat broke. The television and radio were still not reporting everything that people wanted to know, and of course people knew this. According to one opinion poll, half of those questioned said that television, radio, and newspapers were still not informing the public honestly enough. It was

---

* Yuri Andropov (November 1982 to February 1984) and Konstantin Chernenko (February 1984 to March 1985).

also true that nearly two thirds of those polled said that some people were not mature enough to be told everything honestly: no comment. This left consumption: colonial-style cupboards, the weekend house building boom, and porn on VHS tapes smuggled in from abroad. Progress! It was a pleasure that after eight years of hard work, the people of Budapest could finally take possession of the Skála Metró department store. The Miss Europe beauty contest in Vienna welcomed its first-ever Hungarian contestant—and, indeed, she came in third. MOKÉP* opened its first video rental shop in Budapest, and it would not be long before the first sexology conference was held here.

Orwell did not quite envision 1984 being like this. Yet all this was true. Even in Orwell's wildest dreams he would never have imagined that the communists would let a rich American into Hungary and allow him to support whomever he wanted to.

For this was also the year in which the so-called MTA-Soros Foundation Committee was formed.

....

There had never been such a thing in the glorious history of socialism, but this is what was decided. And being "decided" means that it had already been put before Hungary's communist leader János Kádár (who had written "Seen by me" at the bottom of the page). And so it came to pass.

This does raise some questions. In 1984, the Soviet Union was at its peak, and they let in an American uncle. It is very interesting to consider how it was possible, in the mid-1980s, for the communists to agree to the Soros Foundation starting up in Hungary—even if some of the people sitting on its board were members of the Party. Suddenly they allowed the establishment of a registered foundation in Hungary (law under socialism was not familiar with the legal concept of a foundation)—and it was named after an

---

* The state film distributor.

American "imperialist Zionist." A rich American foundation was set up in collaboration with the highest levels of the Party. How was this possible? Why then, why in Hungary, and why Soros?

Sometime in 1983, the phone rang in the apartment of Jani and his family. "Hello, this is George Soros. I'm calling because I want you to be my secretary." Jani was János Betlen, who was then working at the state radio and making a living from translation. He was friends with the liberal opposition figures who, after Hungary joined the IMF and the World Bank, regularly made trips to the West funded by Soros. As he listened to Soros, he thought to himself, "He must be with the CIA, but never mind! America is a democracy. If they want to undermine what's going on here, count me in!"

And why Hungary? Maybe because in the final analysis Hungary was not important. After all was said and done, no one cared about Hungary. It was on the periphery of the two great empires. So why not make it a pilot project—for either the Americans or the Russians? If it failed, one or the other would write off the loss. It would be no big deal.

Perhaps this, or something else, explained why Soros found as his personal representative—his main man, the head of his foundation—someone who was a co-defendant in the trial of Imre Nagy.* But he was someone who survived and was there throughout the whole communist regime: someone who was a Bolshevik, and indeed a high-ranking KGB officer. That someone was Miklós Vásárhelyi. His friends said that his life had been full of twists and turns, struggles, and a thousand experiences, but it was commendable that he had dared to face up to his own weaknesses and mistakes. Well, that was one way of putting it. Vásárhelyi was born in Fiume: Rijeka, in modern-day Croatia. This was also true of János Kádár, who would become the communist

---

* Hungary's prime minister at the time of the 1956 Revolution, who was executed by the Soviets in 1958.

leader of Hungary after 1956; but while Vásárhelyi was born into a bourgeois family, Kádár was born into poverty. Their births were separated by five years, and barely three hundred yards. Vásárhelyi's mother tongue was Italian, he was a fan of AS Roma, and in the 1930s he became an ardent fascist. He later became disillusioned with all that, went down a couple of side roads, and became an ardent communist. After this he became Soros's zealous proconsul in Hungary for many years, up until his death in 2001.

This was the man who introduced Soros to the Bibó István College for Advanced Studies.

....

In fact this was not the college's official name, because that would not have been permitted. In a spirit of rebellion, the students themselves named it after István Bibó, the Hungarian jurist who dreamed of "small circles of freedom," but was forced into silence. It was officially called the "College of Advanced Studies in Law and Social Sciences."

Vásárhelyi visited the young men studying at the college on several occasions, telling them that something interesting was going on: a foundation for the support of independent civil society initiatives had been set up with the help of an American millionaire. Soros would be arriving at some point and Vásárhelyi would bring him to the college, which he might be interested in getting to know. And this is what happened — although perhaps not until 1985.

There must have been thirty people — or forty at most — in the basement room where Fidesz would be formed some years later. No one knew who this man was. All they knew was that he was a rich American with Hungarian roots who wanted to do something in Hungary.

The two of them — Vásárhelyi and Soros — came in. There was nothing ostentatious about Soros, but neither did he give the impression of being an apparatchik. He looked like a gentleman of taste: he wore a sports jacket, which contrasted both with the "comrade gray," besuited world of the Party, and with the sweaters and scuffed shoes typical of members of the intellectual camp in Hungary. There was no hoopla surrounding him: no black Mercedes on the street outside, no bodyguards, no escort party. The meeting was scheduled to last one hour, which turned into two and a half. Soros did not want to leave, and was visibly exhilarated by the encounter.

On the way out he bombarded Vásárhelyi with a string of superlatives describing the students: "Miklós! You're a genius for bringing me here!" The evening left such a deep impression on him that he decided to support the college as it was. This was the future.

One of the smartest of the college students was the leader of a few radicals who wanted to take on the world, and who had already turned the college upside down. This was Orbán. But he was not there that night. Orbán knew that they had an American millionaire coming, but he had no idea who he was. He went to play soccer instead.

Those were the unshaven years. Not only because Orbán was still bearded and had matted hair (he went to the hairdresser once or twice a year, had a buzz cut, and then let it grow), but also because it was the heroic era.

Orbán did not know Soros yet. Soros did not know Orbán yet either (which is why he did not miss him that evening). Neither of them was known to the country at large. We did not yet know, and they did not yet know, that decades later we would need Orbán in order to know who Soros is, and we would need Soros in order for the world to know who Orbán is. At that time Orbán was barely into his twenties, and Soros was in his fifties: an impudent, rebellious student, and an unemotional financial trader with money and power, who nevertheless started their political activities at roughly the same time. This could have been their first meeting. It was not. Yet something was starting to happen.

. . . .

Soros had swung into action. By 1989 the Soros empire had sent a total of 475 into Hungary—no, not tanks, but photocopiers. Apart from the fact that the photocopiers of the time were almost as big as cars, in socialist Hungary these machines were a miracle—and, of course, equivalent to a revolution. The system was terrified of ideas, and of the sharing of ideas. If you put in a piece of paper with an idea on it, within a few moments you had, say, thirty duplicates. Unbelievable! The comrades shook their heads. Wherever photocopiers had even existed before, they were kept behind bars, in locked rooms, and a record was kept of every single page. In the socialist system the photocopier was like the printing press in the Middle Ages: a diabolical machine. Just as Luther produced his "samizdats," the opponents of socialism produced their own inflammatory texts. But the diabolical machine could also be used for diabolical purposes. The spread of the printing press also made possible the spread of the *Malleus maleficarum*—which, to the Devil's annoyance, legalized witch-hunting.* Similarly, Christopher Marlowe's *Doctor Faustus* owed its huge fame to the printing press, with readers of the time finding it entirely plausible that a German scholar would sell his soul to Satan in exchange for twenty-four years of unlimited power and wantonness. So, like the spread of the printing press in the sixteenth and seventeenth centuries, the xerox machine planted the seeds of subversive ideas in the soil of the socialist system. Invitations, programs, pamphlets, books, and previously suppressed articles were reproduced, triggering ferment.

When Soros's photocopier arrived at "Bibó," the alarm was raised immediately. The Party Committee mobilized. They took a good long look at it, because they could not believe what had happened. They drew up rules stating that this diabolical beast had to be placed in a locked room behind a security grille, that security locks had to

---

* "The Hammer of Witches," first published in 1486.

be installed, and that a logbook had to be kept, in which it had to be written down precisely who copied what, in how many copies, and what the content was. And to add a note of frenzy, anyone found breaking these rules would be fired on the spot. Well, the rules were broken, and no one was fired. And the caretaker was kindly asked to take care of nothing.

....

In addition to so-called "equipment procurement," the other nuclear weapon of the "Soros Army" was its scholarship program. The socialist system did not allow young people to be exposed to the influence of capitalism at an early age. Soros broke through this psychological barrier.

One of the first of the Bibó alumni to go to Oxford was József Szájer (followed later by Zsolt Németh from Fidesz, and also Orbán). So what were the Hungarians like? This handful of Hungarians immediately founded the Oxford Hungarian Society. They had good reason to do so, but few are aware that the first documented student of that famous university was also Hungarian: Nicolaus clericus de Hungaria. The Hungarians are a diabolical people, they are everywhere! Szájer came home from England already knowing how a free society operates, and he thought that the following question needed to be asked: Is it really impossible to change the system here at home? Shortly afterwards, this question became the driving force behind Fidesz, which was in the process of being formed: the chances were always stronger than the doubts, and—however slim the hope—it was worth trying.

Others went elsewhere. Attila Várhegyi, for example, went to the United States. There the Hungarians' guide, who had been selected by the US State Department, was a Hungarian émigré who lived in Saint Louis, and who told them that he had to write a report on them every night. This is how they built up their dossiers on the Hungarians. So that is how things went.

A succession of opportunities came and a succession of Hungarians went. Yes, Orbán went to Oxford, but he completed just four months of the nine he had planned to spend at Pembroke College. Politics called him home.

....

Orbán was a separate story. The truth is that from the very beginning everyone was smitten with him. When he spoke up and started talking, everyone took notice. When he went to England, he was sought out by a film crew, and was invited to lunch. After their meal they were forced to conclude that it was not Orbán who had had lunch with them, but they who had had lunch with Orbán.

Orbán was intelligent, courageous, and combative; there were, too, a few more of those ungovernable lads at Bibó College. "Pista" (István Stumpf) could not handle them. Stumpf, the director of the college, was thinking of a career in the Party, and had become the son-in-law of the Interior Minister. Meanwhile the boys were not making things any easier for him. Stumpf always had their backs, but he also thought that these savages had to be civilized, or there would be trouble. So he offered them to János Gyurgyák, to ensure that intellectual work—the editing of the college journal—would occupy their surplus energies.

It did not. They wanted to produce a magazine called *Századvég* ("End of the Century"); but the savages remained savages. On one occasion, Soros sat in on a class Stumpf was giving at the Századvég School of Politics. It was on how a politician should dress. A style expert came in to explain what goes with what and what does not. Soros sat at the back shaking his head. He really did not like what he saw. The reason that he liked this group of people was that they were being themselves, saying what they thought. And now people wanted to teach them how to be like Western politicians.

Soros need not have worried. Orbán knew that you can put on a tie and force yourself into a suit, but you cannot sanitize the inner person. When he talked about this in the mid-1990s, having become a major politician, he said that around him there were no such image-conscious people: they were banished from his circle. Character was all that mattered, that was all that counted!

When they were working on an edition of the magazine focusing on the provincial–metropolitan divide, the sum of what they learned was that everyone should "Buzz off! You too! All you lot! We'll do it our way!"

This became the Fidesz program.

....

The story of Fidesz is one of self-made men. Ten, twenty or thirty men came out of nowhere, flipped up their collars, and wrote their own script. Not only were they considered political nobodies, but geographically most of them were from the middle of nowhere. Orbán was from Felcsút: he was the first in his family to be told that if there was work to be done in the garden and homework, then homework would come first. Orbán understood that everything can be learned and everyone can be learned from. If you are behind the others by a few books, then you read the ten books you are behind by. These are not real problems, they can all be learned. What cannot be learned is character, and in Fidesz strong characters were brought together into a single community. They were people who in every sense came from nowhere, and who felt they could only rely on themselves.

They founded Fidesz—which was a big deal, because the last time students took the initiative in Hungary was back in 1956. Back then they had sparked off a revolution. Now they were preparing to change the course of history once more.

....

In the background was Soros, playing the midwife. Soros supported the college, he funded *Századvég*, and he gave them scholarships. Orbán worked at the Soros-funded

Central Europe Research Group, and his college roommate
Gábor Fodor (no relation to the author) worked at the Soros
Foundation. Later Soros would also support Fidesz. The
fact that Fidesz was able to emerge as a political force in its
own right was in no small part due to Soros's support. With
his help they managed to buy the party's first car, because
until then they had essentially only used private cars; no,
it was not a Trabant, but a dark blue Volkswagen Golf.

At that time the Fidesz men did not know the full story:
all they saw was that Soros was a rich man who gave them
money and asked for nothing in return. The attitude of
Orbán and his circle was that this generation was seizing
an opportunity, and the opportunity was to become players
in Hungarian politics. These young people had already
realized that this was not something that could be learned
in a university course, but that it demanded experience,
time, endeavor, and networking—and Soros was helping
them in all this.

And Soros's strategy was that he had no strategy. Soros
supported everyone—from István Csurka on the Right to
Orbán, and to the liberal SZDSZ. Soros covered all the bases.
He proclaimed that support should be given to anyone
who presented a sensible project and did not simply want
to steal funds. Soros wanted to win over people who were
likely to be major players in Hungarian public life in the
following decades. It was simply that at that point he did
not yet know whom to bet on—and so he bet on everyone,
and kept account of the returns.

When his secretary János Betlen asked him why he had
come to Hungary, Soros told him it was because he calcu-
lated that here a dollar of investment could make a bigger
difference—or, in other words, a bigger profit. Everything
was accounted for in the general ledger. Of course xerox
was a revolution, but that was not why he did it. He spent
dollars on photocopiers, got forints for them in return, and
thus cut out the currency exchange desk at the bank. For
Soros. The photocopier campaign was primarily a currency

exchange issue, and Soros had experience in the foreign exchange market. He was well versed in currency conversion. He even profited from it. Soros never wanted to lose at anything.

....

Soros loved to play tennis. On several occasions his secretary drove him to tennis parties in the Trabant. In the car, Betlen saw that Soros was bracing his legs hard in front of him. "You're afraid, aren't you," Betlen joked, "that the New York Times will run a story about a famous billionaire dying in a plastic box behind the Iron Curtain."

Tennis matches also showed up Soros's fears. He took the game very seriously. When Betlen's ball went over the line, Soros raised his hand in relief to signal that it was out. It was obvious that he really, really did not want to lose. When his secretary pointed this out to him, Soros just said, "Listen! I can't lose, that's the problem. That's how I've made all this money: it's painful to lose, so I'd rather win."

Soros won. When they were coming back, he said to his secretary with a relaxed expression on his face: "I see you're good at handling this little car." Soros appreciated it if things went according to his plans.

1808

....

When a mountain goes to the mountain...

It seemed that the Germans admired Napoleon. The Emperor also met another German giant of the age: Goethe, the author of *Faust*. Goethe believed in stars, destiny, demons, and predestination. He believed that meeting some people brought good luck, while meeting others brought bad luck. He put Napoleon in the former category.

Napoleon knew Goethe's *Werther*, and indeed it was one of his favorite books. When on campaign in Italy he was also inclined to sentimentality, but he cured himself of that quite spectacularly, and — like Goethe — fought hard to ascend to glory. Goethe thought he found genius in dynamism, which he saw as Napoleonic, Caesar-like, seeing the embodiment of it in the execution of great plans.

It was two years after the Battle of Jena. In Erfurt, Napoleon received Goethe for a personal audience. The giant of strength and action met the anointed priest of art and poetry. And legend has it that they saw eye to eye. It is said that at one point in the conversation, the Emperor exclaimed to the author of *Faust*: "Today politics is destiny!" Goethe listed that day among his most cherished.

1 9 8 9

Today politics is destiny. This is the essence of 1989. If you ask anyone in Hungary what happened on June 16, 1989, the only thing they will remember is that Orbán ordered the Russians out of Hungary at Imre Nagy's reburial: "Pack your bags. *Finito*. The party's over." That is when the country, the public, the people of the pubs and bars, first encountered Orbán's name.

Plot 301 (the burial plot for martyrs of the 1956 Revolution in the New Public Cemetery, Budapest): The system was collapsing. When? No day had been assigned. But when free elections took place, at any rate. In the meantime, just one aspect of this process was that the state party was dissolving itself, with its successor party being granted its assets. Kádár died, and George Bush senior visited Hungary. Other political parties already existed. There would be an "opposition roundtable," a referendum, a procession of the Holy Right (the relic of King Saint Stephen) forty-one years after the last one, and free travel—for East Germans too, because we would let them across our western border: freedom. At the same time we were in debt, and they had even admitted that in the past they had lied about the debt, in order to avoid the flight of foreign capital. It was official: the coffers were empty. Unemployment benefits were introduced, the Budapest Stock Exchange opened, and the Hungarian film *Eldorádó* was released.

It was an eventful year, and everything happened so fast.

In the mid-1980s no one would have thought that change would happen here within a few years. It was unimaginable that the overthrow of the communist system might be imminent. Nor did Soros imagine it; he thought it would be a long time coming. He had no intention of overthrowing communism—undermining it, yes, but not overthrowing it.

Neither is it true that he actually overthrew it—even if he told himself that and said so, or believed it. But he was firmly convinced that he had won. Back then he talked a lot about how he had achieved great things with very little money, and how it felt very good to have defeated evil.

He was smarter than the communists. He proudly confessed that he had collaborated with them. The communists had wanted to exploit him, and Soros had wanted to exploit them. By his own admission that was the basis of the collaboration—and he had won.

An astonishing scene took place on Hungarian television's New Year's Eve show in 1989. Soros answered questions put to him by three comedians while he peeled potatoes. One of them said to him, "Wherever you set foot, five years later the system collapses." To this Soros replies, "Does it take that long?" The audience laughs.

Soros felt he had arrived, he was home, he had overthrown communism, and everything here was his: without him there was nothing here. He never imagined that the youngster who made history in front of hundreds of thousands of people on that Budapest square—and who others say overthrew communism—would years later think to himself: "If I've sent the Russians home, I'll send Uncle George home too."

....

In 1989 Orbán was asked on TV: "Do we need to be serious about you lot?" Orbán replied, "Deadly serious."

....

A few years later János Betlen—by then Soros's former secretary—gave Orbán a strange trinket as a birthday present: the red fob used on the key for the party's lakeside property number 301 in the Hungarian resort of Balatonaliga. It bore this inscription: "MSZP. Ice-cold Coca-Cola, the Real Thing Protected by Law!"

So much for 1989.

1990

By the 1980s everyone was fed up to the back teeth with communism. Almost everyone could tell you why they did not want it: I do not want it because you cannot buy good jeans here, I am not allowed to wear my hair long, and the music is terrible. After the Soviet Union, everyone was especially fed up with Russians. But America was attractive. Very attractive: Route 66, rock and roll, Coca-Cola. And then permission was given for *Dallas* to be broadcast in Hungary. Our image of life in America was, "I've got a swimming pool or two." We nurtured a dream image of America.

So after 1990 the Soviet Union collapsed and nothing was left of it here: everyone wanted everything American, and Western Europe was in the ascendant. What we saw there were very high living standards, freedom, and everything we wanted. In 1990 the only task we had was to become like the West as soon as possible. Only after very many years did it become clear that the West was changing, and that we were changing too: both we and the West became moving targets.

But America had the privilege of a fantastic insight, one which eventually took the Russians down: this was the realization that the most important weapon is soft power. What arrived here was not only jeans, fizzy drinks, McDonald's (the first "meki" in Budapest opened in 1986), American films, and idiot-proof narratives of right and wrong. What also arrived was Soros.

Soros was the embodiment of soft power: manifest virtue and philanthropy; selfless, generous support for benign initiatives; the strengthening of civil society; freedom, openness, and democracy; and, of course, the fight against evil dictatorships. Soros was the unrelenting fight of good against evil. And this morality tale worked. Soros bought the intelligentsia, he brought the talking heads within his orbit, and he made a generous offer to anyone who was open to it. The intelligentsia were grateful, and did not have to think twice: it was all for a good cause, they were given money, all the resources they needed, scholarships, and university posts. They drank deep from the punch bowl, while the tale of philanthropy was spun to the people. And, as with *Dallas*, everyone loved it.

So America invented Soros, built a story around him, and built the network. And we were the pilot project.

. . . .

Soros's life is full of unanswered questions. How did he get his money? He told his secretary that after he went to London he worked in a bank. They saw he was staying late, and he had ideas about how to do this and that. The ideas were taken on, he was given a lot of money, and then more. The rest is history.

How did he get his degree? He cannot have graduated from high school. He left Hungary at the age of seventeen (in 1947), obviously not having gone to school in the final years of the war. He had even planned to attend university in the Soviet Union, because he thought communism was important and wanted to understand how it worked. But did he even go to university? We do not know. We do not know how he got his degree from the London School of Economics. Nor do we know in what capacity he attended lectures by his mentor, Karl Popper, whether he attended other courses, or whether he took any exams at all. János Betlen, his former secretary, was convinced that Soros had not completed a single course in full.

Soros wanted to be a philosopher, but he had to postpone that project because first he needed to make a lot of money. Well, *c'est la vie*. He has written a lot of unreadable books (the first in 1990, on the opening up of the Soviet system). Soros has proved to be a lousy philosopher.

Then there were the American years. In 1969 he took out a loan of four billion dollars to found a company which just over a decade later was worth a hundred billion dollars. There were years in which his hedge funds made him a

profit of over 100 percent. Such things are too fantastic to
even feature in tales. Obviously it can only be done through
insider trading, the intelligence services, and offshore activity.

Yet Soros was fond of talking—everywhere, and to everyone—about his huge financial successes, and about how he
was a bellwether, a guru, a messiah. He is the unseen mover,
who with his financial tricks brings down currencies and
national economies. Just some of the currencies Soros has
attacked: the French franc, the British pound, the German
mark, the Thai baht, the Malaysian ringgit, the Russian
ruble, and the Hungarian forint. And with his political
activities he punishes hardcore dictatorships. Soros sees
himself as the God of the Old Testament: "benevolent,
invisible, but all-seeing." When this "god" is casually asked
about the details of how he does it, his answer is usually
just this: "I remember the future." Obviously this is a rea-
sonably astute answer if one does not want to be tripped
up by contradictions in one's own mythology.

Then Hungary became not only a pilot project, but also
a prototype. By 1992, the franchise had been taken to twenty-
two countries, and by 1993 to thirty-one. Today there are
Soros foundations or organizations of some kind in nearly
one hundred and fifty countries. So Soros is without doubt
a Goliath.

....

He is also a Goliath among speculators. Legend has it that
Soros is a self-made billionaire: he did not inherit a fortune,
but became one of the richest men in the world through
his own efforts and talent. He is certainly clever and has a
talent for making money; but the validity of the qualifier
"self-made" is debatable.

Even by his own admission, he has made his fortune
through speculation, shady deals, insider information, and
unregulated markets. He did not even like paying taxes. He
also set up his international organization, the Open Society
Foundations, to indulge in a little "optimization." Over

the years he has damaged quite a few national economies:
"Oh gosh, that's life! You should have been on your guard!"

On several occasions Soros has stated, with a straight
face, that the possibility for speculation playing the role
it plays—which happens to be destructive—is the fault
of the system. According to this, speculation is a natural
thing. Its conquests are due to the fact that it generates
profit. Profit is the ultimate meaning of things. Morality is
not part of the game. For if, God forbid, one should ever
have moral doubts about what one is doing, these moral
considerations would incessantly influence and thus limit
one's behavior in the pursuit of profit. This must not be
allowed; it is absolutely *verboten!*

International investments dissolve borders and currencies, and destroy lives, but this has no moral significance
whatsoever. In the financial markets one is not confronted
with moral issues; finding oneself in such a situation would
be like fighting with one's hands tied behind one's back.
And another question is what kind of people are involved
in this activity. The money-makers in the money markets
are anonymous: they are invisible, without morals, and
without names. In this sense there is no Soros. He who
intervenes, speculates, seeks profit, and creates mayhem
is not Soros, but some anonymous agent: a "phantom."
It does not matter who he is. If he did not do these things,
someone else would; and so it is better if he does it.

. . . .

When being interviewed once, Soros said that in certain
situations he would prick up his ears and would feel saliva
forming in his mouth. He felt drawn to those deals that
arise in a state of disequilibrium: the greater the chaos,
the bigger the profit. Soros was very concerned about what
would happen after the fall of communism. Of all the former
communist countries, Hungary was in the worst economic
situation. Under the Kádár regime, the debt per capita
was by far the highest in the region. Inflation was high,

the standard of living was in decline, real wage levels were falling, and unemployment had become a visible reality. The national debt had grown to twenty-one billion euros, but at the time the exact figure was still unclear. All that was known was that it was immense. Hungary was on the verge of meltdown, threatened by instability and chaos. And Soros liked situations like that. So he pricked up his ears and salivated.

He volunteered to take on Hungary's entire national debt. In return, "all" he asked for was the transfer to him of Hungarian industry: the more valuable part of the nation's wealth. "Business as usual." But József Antall, our first freely elected prime minister, resisted. Then, over the years, Soros repeatedly stalked the largest Hungarian retail bank, OTP. He wanted to buy it out at a knock-down price and then use it to finance his university. But Antall's successor Peter Boross also resisted. There was even resistance from Gyula Horn, the leader of the subsequent socialist (MSZP) government. He said he wouldn't let a capitalist in. For this reason Soros could not stand Horn. "This was not the deal. I didn't start operations here just to have my plans blocked!" Soros was riled.

. . . .

Hungary was the first place where Soros experimented with building a network that could advance his personal interests as effectively as possible. It was here that he developed his magic phrases, such as "creating equal opportunities," "the Roma program," and "human rights violations." And it was here that he launched his philanthropic activities, the purchase of hospital equipment, a school milk program, and various scholarship programs. The aim was to set up his own network in line with deceptive, seemingly innocent goals, drawing in people he could win over. His strategy was to bet on everyone, support everyone who approached him, and fund everyone he could.

But among the equals there were those who were more equal. Soros's real darling was the liberal SZDSZ, and this fact became very strongly and deeply embedded in the subconscious of Fidesz. Fidesz felt that the SZDSZ had been overindulged. They saw it as a sign of their own strength that they could have received that support, that they could have "won that lottery," and then they would have been where the SZDSZ was — or could even have knocked them out. At the same time they were filled with a kind of defiant pride that they had been able to get where they were through their own efforts.

So in Fidesz there was a kind of unconscious frustration with the SZDSZ: an impatience with the way in which the whole SZDSZ spirit was being transferred into Hungarian cultural life, and an irritation with the fact that they were trying to dominate Hungarian culture. The SZDSZ thought that here at last was a testing ground on which the bourgeois radicalism of the early twentieth-century politician Oszkár Jászi could be put into practice. This was pure communist logic: they saw the country as a testing ground, and felt that their time had come. They were in exactly the right place at the right time: in a country devastated by the fall of the previous system, where they could execute their own project.

After their honeymoon period, the SZDSZ felt that with Fidesz they had caught a Tartar. At first they thought that Orbán and co. would carry things forward in the way they wanted (Antall, Csurka, and their associates thought so too), but then they were disappointed. So here were these wolves in sheep's clothing derailing the project. Their plan would fail because of Fidesz: not because of the post-communists, but because of Orbán and his people.

From the very beginning, Fidesz was in grave danger of being swallowed up by the SZDSZ. It was even said that if the SZDSZ was a worm, then Fidesz was its tail. In particular it was Gábor Fodor, Orbán's college roommate, who argued for the formation of a liberal bloc, because of the hopelessness of the policies of Antall *et al.* The argument was that the momentum, strength, and popularity of Fidesz should be combined with the organization of the SZDSZ, and the feeling that they were the ones whose time had arrived—something which, by the way, would matter a lot to the electorate. But from Orbán's point of view this would involve giving up Fidesz's independence. This is why he broke off his course in Oxford on a Soros scholarship. He had to come home to bring order to the ranks of Fidesz and prevent its absorption by the SZDSZ.

Orbán was all along in favor of maintaining independence—from everyone. He repeatedly told his friends that they could decide to sell the party, so to speak, and then go in whatever direction the decision took them; that is what it would cost, but he did not recommend that, because they could only maintain their integrity if they remained independent of everyone. In relation to Soros, Orbán clearly saw that there was no need to be coy: opportunities should be taken when offered, but nothing should be owed by either side to the other. This in itself was considered an outrageous position. The SZDSZ, who were in Soros's debt and had made a Faustian bargain with him, always said that Fidesz were ungrateful. Orbán and his circle did not even understand why they should be grateful.

According to Soros, everyone could be bought. But Orbán was not for sale.

1862

....

This was the year of the publication of the most influential work in Hungarian drama, *The Tragedy of Man*.* Even if we did not know if from anywhere else, we know from this work that the Devil is always tempting us. He comes in different forms, but always in the image of what is good. This is a fact. So the Devil is the Great Deceiver, but the fabric concealing him always wears thin, and the silhouette revealed is that of Lucifer. This always happens throughout history, and this is probably the order of things.

What is God doing? God says, "I am steering with a steady hand what needs to be steered. I leave many things for people to decide for themselves. It is a matter for them whether what they decide is right or wrong."

God sees what the Devil is doing (we can call it the bad within people, evil, or whatever is demonic). And as He must somehow govern the world, He must find some way to counteract this—and He always finds some instrument with which to do this. Because He knows that he always has to fight the Devil.

---

* The most famous play in the Hungarian language, by Imre Madách. Its main characters are Adam, Eve, and the Devil, Lucifer.

1992

Orbán spent six weeks in America on a German Marshall Fund grant. After a preliminary training course in Washington, DC, he headed for New York. Then, together with a number of leading members of Fidesz, he held major talks with leading US officials. This was a major coup for a small party from "a country which I couldn't find on a map." This was also when Orbán finally met Soros. Soros's offices in New York were on Columbus Circle, near Central Park, the center of the globalist world. Soros invited the Fidesz organizers to meet him at the very top, on the top floor. For Orbán, it was like when Satan tempted Christ, saying to him, "Here is the world at your feet; here it is, you can have it." Orbán looked down from the sixtieth floor and, indeed, there before him was the world. Soros praised how well they were fighting in Hungary, saying that if they kept it up, they would meet with success (in the polls at the time Fidesz were leading by a large margin, by forty percent, and in their minds they must have been preparing to govern). Soros also said that he really liked what Orbán and his team were doing, which was why he had decided that from then on he would cover all the costs which were necessary to ensure their victory. This was the offer.

So Soros tried to make a deal with the party most expected to win. Of course for Orbán and his circle this was extremely flattering, but he also sensed that this was going to be a problem. Because Soros obviously wanted to gain influence over the next government—something which he had completely failed to achieve with regard to the Antall government at that time. Having been put on the spot, Orbán came out with the following: "It's very good that you've spoken so highly of our work, but at home we're so successful that we're flush with money: we have everything, and we don't need a penny. People are so supportive that we don't need any extra funding—but if we ever do, we'll gladly take you up on this generous offer." With this, Orbán disarmed Soros.

When they were in the elevator on their way down József Szájer called Orbán to account: "But Viktor, we're flat broke, we don't have a penny, and Soros would have given us money!" Orbán replied, "But what would he have asked for in return? Believe me, Józsi, there's no such thing as a free lunch!"

Orbán's thinking was sound. He knew that there was no way to get money without having to pay it back in some way. Or in other words: if you accept Soros's money, you have to follow his orders. To Orbán this was unacceptable. In politics the most important thing is autonomy, the ability to act independently, and anyone who surrenders that is surrendering himself. Orbán felt that God had solved the matter.

Orbán was also under no illusions: after the temptation in New York, he knew that Soros had added him to his little black book of enemies. But he was smart enough to say, "I'm not stupid either! If someone adds me to his black book of enemies, I'd better add him to mine." There is a page for those who must be given "the bread of adversity and the water of affliction," on which Orbán has written the name: "George Soros." From then on there were two little black books, and the situation was clear.

. . . .

At a dinner in Budapest Soros would receive a message similar to that received by Orbán at the meeting in New York.

István Csurka had already written his famous essay, "Some Thoughts on the Two Years Since the Fall of Communism and the New Program of the MDF," which was published in *Magyar Fórum* on August 20, 1992. This had raised the specter of "fascism," and made it necessary to decide where to stand. Soros invited some Fidesz members to dinner at the Kisbíró Restaurant in Budapest. The Kisbíró was one of those restaurants with a popular and highly regarded chef, but Orbán did not know this at the time, because these Fidesz party leaders did not have the money to go to such places. To this day, if he closes his eyes Orbán can picture how the tail of a zander was curled up in the large dish in front of him. During the dinner Soros presented his analysis of Hungary. He said that there was now a danger of fascism, that it was on the march. The current government was unable to stop it, because the idea had infiltrated the ruling party, and so a change of government was definitely needed in the next election. Or sooner if possible. Therefore Fidesz's hostility towards the MSZP needed to be abandoned, because the SZDSZ—which comprised so many intelligent people—had already accepted the necessity of working with the former communists. Fidesz alone remained radically anti-communist. Fidesz alone was unable to see beyond the past and beyond communism, and did not yet understand that there was a much greater danger. So, like it or not, it had to work with the post-communists. Soros started from the premise that he had won the battle against communist dictatorship, but if things continued in the way they were going, he would lose the battle against Nazi dictatorship; and that could not be allowed to happen.

Orbán and his team were utterly outraged by the offer, but interestingly the most vehement response did not come from Orbán, or even László Kövér,* but Klára Ungár—who a year later would defect to the SZDSZ. She quite simply sent Soros to hell: "What the hell do you think you're doing? We're in politics to get rid of the commies! You come here and tell us to throw in our lot with the *ancien régime!* This is complete nonsense!"

Soros did not like that very much. He considered the return of the Nazi Arrow Cross Party** to be a real danger. Far-right hell-raising was coming back—not only in Hungary, but across the whole region. So the three opposition parties would have to work together: the empire of evil on

---

* A founding member of Fidesz and the current speaker of the National Assembly of Hungary.
** In power in Hungary from October 1944 to March 1945, during the country's occupation by Nazi Germany.

the other side had come together, so the empire of good
would have to come together. Two worlds had come into
conflict. Those who belonged to one world had to stand
here with us, and those who belonged to the other world
had to stand over there. And, as Soros saw it, Orbán had
not stood here, but over there.

For a long time after this there was no meeting between
them, and the reason was that after such a meeting there
was nothing further to discuss.

....

So the confrontation did not begin with migration, not
in 2015, not with the billboards of Soros in 2017: it began
much earlier, in the heroic era, when the two protagonists
in our story already felt that the conflict between them was
irreconcilable, and its causes were fundamental.

Initially, it seemed that Orbán and Soros were on the
same side: both aimed to create a free world in opposition
to the communist dictatorship. Orbán and his associates
were fighting for freedom, for the right to self-determination,
for national sovereignty, for the overthrow of the communist
system; and Soros was supporting them in this. The arch-
enemy, the communists, had the material power; Fidesz
had nothing, and it was from this perspective that they
saw Soros.

And then, very slowly, the fabric was exposed, and began
to wear thin. Soros wanted access to political power, he
wanted access to the nation's wealth, and he wanted to make
a profit. Soros was not driven by the desire to strengthen
national sovereignty, but by something else entirely. It was
just that these raw interests and goals had been given a
sugar coating: "open society," "philanthropy," "freedoms,"
and so on. History, however, had rendered Orbán's circle
and their generation resistant to such sleights of hand, and
they immediately saw the ulterior motives behind the fine-
sounding rhetoric. Orbán was courageous and farsighted
enough to not only want to say no to temptation, but to

be able to say no to it. Think of the audacity of it! There was this rich, powerful, effective global network of foundations with openly stated political aims, backed by the most powerful country in the world and its entire arsenal. This was what he had to say no to. Not many people have been able to do such a thing.

But even Soros had to take a step back. Soros would have bet on Orbán, but Orbán did not bet on Soros. And this has had obvious consequences. So Orbán has been an obstacle. Soros went here, there, and everywhere, trying to gain access to political power; but Antall, our first freely elected Prime Minister, resisted and blocked his path. And Antall's actions have always been reference points for Orbán. Antall's Hungarian Democratic Forum (MDF) did not yield to Soros; and as Fidesz was preparing to inherit the MDF's place in Hungarian politics, the question of whether to cooperate with Soros became one of political identity.

This created a hidden discourse that has never been written in texts on Hungarian political history. It was not written anywhere, but everyone knew, it was in everyone's head, that the other side were serving foreign interests and we were the ones not serving those interests. From Orbán's point of view, this was the defining fault line in Hungarian politics.

....

There were those who collaborated with Soros. Soros had a strong presence in Hungary. In a poor country that had hardly enough resources to spend on culture, education, and research, Soros was a king. Some people sought his favor and flattered him; and Soros rewarded them if they did what he asked. But those who resisted, who bridled, were sidelined by him, threatened and accused.

The SZDSZ was grateful. It was the party, and its loyalists were the people, who benefited disproportionately from Soros's support. In return they rendered unto Caesar what was Caesar's. The so-called "Demszky dinners" were legendary (named after the long-serving SZDSZ Mayor of Budapest). Soros's arrival at Budapest City Hall was frequently like the arrival of the Sun King: he was greeted with courtly humility by his subjects, who listened to his words and watched his steps, lest he stumble on the red carpet.

Soros really felt that this was his country, where he was king. It was no accident that this was where he set up his university. One of Soros's biggest projects was undoubtedly the establishment of Central European University (CEU) in Prague in 1991, which took place with the support of then-President of Czechoslovakia Václav Havel. Soros originally wanted the university to be located in Bratislava, and he envisaged the future Slovak parliament building as its headquarters. But Slovak intellectuals found it unacceptable for a building that was important to them to be owned by a billionaire of Hungarian origin. So alongside Budapest Soros chose Prague; but with the break-up of Czechoslovakia in 1993 and the election of Václav Klaus as Prime Minister of the Czech Republic, a new government, opposed to Soros, radically reduced state support for CEU. Soros made his decision: in 1994 CEU moved its forward operating base permanently and completely to Budapest. With this, everything fell into place.

CEU was a training camp, a training center for the whole Central European region, for the region's elite gladiator corps of future prime ministers. Soros's vision was that its first students would all be trained to be prime ministers, and then go on to implement the transitions that were needed in their home countries. Everyone was told that they were there because they were talented, and because their knowledge and capabilities were better than those of others. And this is where all the big shots from the SZDSZ taught—for salaries that were incomparably higher than others in Hungary. They offered a socialization channel (and a narrative) to the students of the Soros University. It was just a matter of whether they could identify with this; those who could were the ones who were selected.

There was undoubtedly a massive indoctrination program underway at the Soros University. People there were fed the idea that human rights exist, and that therefore they must take precedence over national sovereignty (the support of human rights obviously means internationalism). Most of the teachers believed that the cause of conflict in the world is nationalism, and that duty to the nation is a harmful and evil phenomenon which needs to be consigned to history. Therefore, in the interest of greater freedom, they said, limits must be imposed on the absolute power of nation-states. It was a moral duty to open the gate and intervene to enforce the principles of justice. For if the question was one of what we owe one another and whether we should support the downtrodden of the world or the downtrodden in our own community, then the right answer was the downtrodden of the world. For Soros's people, their natural community was not a nation-state, but humanity as a whole. They felt, they taught, they drummed into the heads of the students here, that borders must lose their significance, and that the aim was not only to replace non-democratic governments with democratic governments, but also to replace nation-states with international institutions and outsource the role of the state to civil-society organizations. They also drew up the moral indictment against the nation: commitment to the nation-state, ethno-radicalism, was the cause of the greatest evil imaginable — that of anti-Semitism.

The Soros legion's anti-Semitism project was specifically aimed at deepening and entrenching the concept of the "guilty nation," with the further objective that — whatever happened in the world — Hungarians and Hungarian nationalism must not be given absolution. The curriculum was thus centered around an unquenchable hatred, which presented the Hungary of Miklós Horthy — the country's leader in the interwar period and the early years of the Second World War — as even guiltier than the Germans of that time. They showed immense determination in building this narrative, which, decades later, would lay the intellectual foundations for cancel culture. It was also intended to make possible the promotion of a utopian vision for the creation of a new social order in which the greatest imaginable human evil, as seen to have existed under Horthy, could no longer occur, as its facilitating human structure—the nation-state—would, of necessity, be superseded, defeated, shattered, and forced open.

. . . .

1992. This was the year when Soros launched an astonishing large-scale attack on a national currency: the British pound. On September 16 every passing hour saw more of the British taxpayer's savings being siphoned off into Soros's pockets. Every five minutes he made as much money as an average American family earns in a year of work. That speculative attack on the pound made Soros one billion dollars, of which he transferred 250 million to CEU.

For Soros, '92 was a particularly good year.

1944

Perhaps the happiest year of Soros's life. This is what he has said himself.

Soros is an old man, in his mid-nineties, and he lived through the Holocaust here in Hungary. He had faith in himself and in his father that nothing bad could happen to him. And nothing bad happened to him.

Despite his provocative statement that this was perhaps the happiest time of his life, we can believe his assertion that what happened to him in Hungary back then was a truly defining experience.

The Holocaust taught him that the principle of the nation is a menace. The historical experience of the Jews of Central Europe was that they had "no homeland." The nation and the Hungarian community did not protect them from deportation, and they had to protect themselves as best they could. They found that they could not trust the domestic political elite either, because it was "fascistizing." Moreover, nation-states not only failed to protect the Jews, but paved the road to hell for them. Thus the principle of the nation-state is seen to be a diabolical one.

These experiences find echoes in Soros's political perceptions, which in fact are driven by fear: fear of the "closedness" of European nations, with their cultural and communal foundations; and fear of "irrational" political elites—principally right-wing, of course—unfettered by checks and balances. Soros's globalized, supranational liberalism is therefore really afraid of two things: right-wing governments, because they are "Nazis"—even if they deny it; and people, who are savages, and who—through their prejudices and racism—become "Nazis" themselves in certain circumstances.

What is most absurd about Soros's idea is that (supranational) liberal democracy must be protected from both the political elite and the voters themselves. This concept is still reflected in the criticism of Hungary today, which takes aim at both the "corrupt," "fascistizing," "Nazi" right-wing elite and the "racist" Hungarian in the street.

This also explains why Soros, as a Jew, has no sympathy for the Jewish nation-state of Israel. The reason is that it is based on the national principle, and therefore—paradoxically—can even be called "Nazi." His own supranational organizations are often critical of the Israeli leadership, thus provoking Israel's displeasure. From this perspective, Soros is one of the biggest financial sponsors of anti-Israel, anti-Jewish, anti-Semitic NGOs—both in the West and in Israel itself. Even in the Israel–Hamas conflict that erupted in 2023, it is Soros who organizes and funds almost all the violent pro-Palestinian protests in major European cities and liberal American universities. It is no accident that in Israel he has become *persona non grata*.

In any case, this does not stop Soros from playing the anti-Semitism card in his own defense. Anyone who attacks Soros is an anti-Semite. And that is a powerful card that trumps every other. There is no defense against it.

But this is also where Soros learned that in abnormal circumstances you cannot play by the rules of normality. If you do, you will lose. This is fundamental in both business and politics. If there is no norm, then everything is allowed, and you become the norm yourself. Here is a very important Soros rule.

. . . .

The year that Soros calls the happiest of his life saw the completion of a book that would have a defining influence on Soros's entire public life: the now classic work *The Open Society and its Enemies*, by the world-famous Austrian-born Jewish philosopher Karl Popper.

This is where Soros got the name of his foundation and his organizations: "Open Society." Hence the critique of "closed societies" (the aversion to communist and nationalist regimes), the formulation of the desired goal (global, supranational "liberal democracy"), and the philosophical justification for the means used to achieve it (direct and indirect intervention).

At the same time, there is a line of thought in this book that explains the essence of the opposition between Orbán and Soros.

Although Orbán and Soros have always handled the conflict between them in a civil and gentlemanly way, in fact this conflict has been insoluble from the beginning, and this is due to a single sentence or thought. According to Popper's line of thought, someone who thinks that their country represents something special, and therefore puts their own country first, is thereby already establishing a dictatorship. This in itself is an outrageous statement, and an anthropological absurdity, as we tend to think that every person thinks that his or her own country is the best and the most important—or, if not, that he or she must work to make it so. This absurdity is the position that Soros occupies.

Orbán is the polar opposite. He believes that God created not only humans but also nations, and that it is written that nations will be either damned or glorified: they will be judged. Every nation is a lineament on the face of all mankind, which is made in the image and likeness of God. In other words, a nation is a sacred thing, a creation of value worth fighting for, and it is good if this creation of value is never lost. Those who work for it are good, and those who reject it are bad.

Behind the confrontation between Orbán and Soros, therefore, lies a fundamental conflict that has anthropological depth—and, consequently, metaphysical depth. Therefore the conflict between the two is irreconcilable. There can be no compromise; the conflict signifies utter incompatibility, and there is no chance of rapprochement. So, Orbán or Soros: one or the other.

In metaphysical terms—or even more so in theological terms—it is like the struggle between the Angel and the Devil, between the forces that protect the order of creation and the forces that subvert it. In Orbán's eyes, Soros is "the Great Disruptor"—a name, together with "the Old Gentleman," used in the Middle Ages to refer to the Devil. According to Orbán, everything that people like us think is important to assemble and build is what Soros thinks is worthy of disruption—and he will do his best to disrupt it.

If we think of our lives, and if we want to die believing in a few things, then Soros is undoubtedly the man who will seek to convince you that it all makes no sense. There is no point in believing in anything, he will say, and there is no point to your life other than living it as pleasantly as possible. It is nonsensical to seek a higher purpose or meaning in it. This is why he wants to rob you of your identity—because any higher purpose or meaning flows from your identity. If you happen to be a man, then you have a mission which involves having children with a woman, loving them, and taking care of them. Therefore it means something to your life that you were born a man. Being born Hungarian is a calling, a mission, a task. We were born here, and the task that fate has given us must be completed. It is a moral duty to preserve, strengthen, and carry forward in this place a thousand-year-old civilization, built with the Hungarian language and based on Hungarian traditions. And if you are also a follower of Christ, then another task for you is building the Kingdom of God.

But what Soros is saying is that whether you are a man or not is unimportant. Why you were born a Hungarian is irrelevant, and God either is long dead or never existed at all. End of story. All that Soros stands for is ultimately summed up in an intellectual trend based on the proposition that in the end life will come to nothing anyway. And if in the end it comes to nothing, if it is futile, then it is completely pointless to set goals which demand suffering, fighting, or sacrifices from you. "Nothing" is what Soros proposes to you as the thread of life. And "nothing" is strong—very strong.

Of course Soros thinks that he stands for something: the spread of freedom itself, and the potential for a new world to be built around very important values that will protect us from the dangers posed by closed societies. Ultimately, what will protect us is not tradition, but the liberal values, supranational institutions, and "civil oversight" promoted by Soros: not shared culture, not accepted morality, not language, not families, not nation states, not democracy, and certainly not elected leaders. This is why, for the greater good, they can all be attacked, destroyed, undermined, deleted. If there are no norms, then everything is permitted, and you become the norm.

So it is not just a case of two people who will oppose each other: what are in conflict are two worldviews, two intellectual forces, and two political positions. At the root of all this is that the view of humans and human nature held by the "Orbánists" is very different from that of the "Sorosists."

Neither is the struggle between these two concepts or world forces new; it is just that now it is embodied in two Hungarians. The struggle itself has existed at least since the unified Christian worldview lost its monopoly. The source of this is in the idea that since in the end we are going to die, we frame this as a problem and make it the focus of our thinking. These thoughts are then assembled into philosophies and political views, and in the political space parties are created, based on this diversity. In fact, this is the beginning of the modern political world.

Although these are important — even fundamental — issues, we do not talk about them today, or hardly at all — although we should. The reason we do not talk about them is that in the Western world today there is a prevailing perception of the "meaninglessness of such issues," which goes hand in hand with the hollowing out of intellectual debate, the disappearance of thought, the marginalization of political leaders, and the bureaucratization of political issues. Specifically, the reason the Western world today does not pay attention to these issues is that a liberal does not address them.

This is the world that Orbán has challenged.

1994

As it became clear that Fidesz and Orbán could not be bought, they began to be frozen out. The effect was not direct and immediate, but one could see why it was happening. The "problem" with Orbán was that he had forged his own path and did not take instructions from outside. Soros simply had no influence over Fidesz.

Therefore Soros resorted to other tactics. These were not specific attempts at interference, such as we have seen recently, for example, with US intervention in the Polish elections. They were instead attempts at destabilization of a strategic nature.

These are strategies for the positioning of others, not their elimination. Soros's intention is to fix the positions of the various players, to pin everyone down in what he sees as their right place. In these operations, however, Orbán has always been the odd man out. After his speech at Imre Nagy's reburial, it must have become abundantly clear to Soros that Orbán was in a separate category, and that Orbán could spell trouble for him. This is why the "top dog"—Soros himself—made Orbán an offer, instead of leaving it to an underling. Soros could already see that Orbán had outstanding skills: he saw that he was smart and determined, and that he was a serious opponent.

So right from the start there was a plan for Fidesz to be brought under the wing of the SZDSZ, and for the latter to be ready to join forces with the socialists, if the situation so required.

When Orbán was studying at Oxford under Timothy Garton Ash,* Gábor Fodor gave an interview in which he laid down his gun and acknowledged that Fidesz and the SZDSZ should work together. When he heard this,

---

* A British historian, author, and commentator who is currently Professor of European Studies at the University of Oxford.

Orbán packed his bags and came home. If he had not come home, the SZDSZ would certainly have devoured Fidesz. As László Kövér said at the time, "We will deal with our enemies somehow, but Lord, save us from our friends." Orbán and his team thought that their real opponent was not the ruling MDF, but the SZDSZ, which feigned a friendly embrace.

Since it was clear that the coalition would not work, because the Fidesz leaders would not submit, there were ever more attempts at destabilization. Fidesz had a massive lead in the polls, when, suddenly, out of nowhere, an attack came from within one of its congresses: there was a demand that the leadership should be dismissed, because it could not account for the party's funds. Then the press got to work, with an increasing number of articles saying that people should be afraid of Orbán, because if he gained power there would be a dictatorship. They demonized Orbán. And in a fight against the Devil, no weapons are off-limits. They tried to undermine Orbán in whatever way they could, with the aim of creating tension within Fidesz. For example, they looked everywhere for someone who would run against Orbán to become party president, and then that would be the end of Orbán. But they should have known that it is only worth attempting a coup if it is successful.

. . . .

There was a movement called the Democratic Charter, the purpose of which was to bring the SZDSZ and the post-communists together. Originally the Charter was mobilized by some SZDSZ politicians: the idea came from the philosopher János Kis and the novelist György Konrád. Their declared intention was to defend the democratic commitment of the people against the rise of the "far right." The leaders of the SZDSZ saw the Antall government as a threat to democracy, and said that the opposition parties had a duty to take joint action against it.

Therein lay the problem.

From 1990 until the founding of the Democratic Charter, the post-communists were in quarantine, and no one
cooperated with them: they were communists, and therefore
lepers. Then suddenly Iván Vitányi of the MSZP and the
post-communists were invited to Budapest's Merlin Theatre
for their first major meeting. This slowly brought them out
of their isolation.

József Antall sacked György Surányi, the Governor of the
Hungarian National Bank—and not coincidentally one of
Soros's key men, who had signed the Democratic Charter.
Following this, the grand plan was set in motion, with
street demonstrations, and the communists also speaking
out "in defense of democracy." Fidesz were no longer a part
of this. For Orbán and his party the penny had dropped:
an anti-fascist popular front was being created to bridge
the division between anti-communists and communists,
forming the basis for an alliance of the parties on both
sides of the divide.

Fidesz did not agree to this. From then on it was "Cry
'Havoc!' and let slip the dogs of war." No quarter was given.
Every accusation was deployed: dictatorship, corruption,
the party headquarters affair, the schism, anti-Semitism.
A carpet-bombing campaign began, which by 1994 had
almost brought down Fidesz and had produced a coalition
of anti-communists and post-communists.

. . . .

Attempts to destabilize the party at levels below Orbán
were also well underway.

When Zsolt Bayer, the proud owner of Fidesz Mem-
bership Book Number 5, started his career as a journalist
and wrote the article *Éjjeli nap* ("Night Sun") in response
to Sándor Csoóri's *Nappali hold* ("Daytime Moon"), he got
amiable pats on the head from established writers such as
Tamás Ungvári and Mihály Kornis. Ungvári called Bayer:
"Zsolti, you're one of the young generation of journalists,
please decide whether you want to go to the USA or Japan

on a scholarship for eighteen months or two years. I'm talking about those places because I can get you in there." Then, just as Orbán was judged to have gone over to the dark side, Bayer became a Nazi bastard, and no one went to him any more asking where he wanted to go on a Soros scholarship. But he would be called for another reason: Kornis contacted him, saying that no one can stay out of the provincial–metropolitan debate; and that if he did not remain on their side (the good side, the metropolitans), he needed to realize that he would become a Nazi, and that he would never again be either a journalist or a writer in Hungary.

So Bayer became a "Nazi."

Perhaps he was the first of the Fidesz folk to be smeared as an anti-Semite, and perhaps the first domino to fall: "If Orbán's friend is anti-Semitic, and Orbán doesn't distance himself from him, then Orbán's anti-Semitic. Since he's a founder of Fidesz and anti-Semitic, if he's not fired, then the whole of Fidesz is anti-Semitic." So you do not have to do anti-Semitic things to be anti-Semitic. You can be anti-Semitic even if you are not anti-Semitic: you just need to be accused, say, of not doing everything—or not doing enough—to combat rising anti-Semitism. The anti-Semitic card has become the ace of trumps, which can win every trick.

But in the beginning, when there was talk of merging with the SZDSZ, it was not like that. Back then the opposite was true: the party had been branded "Zsidesz" (a conflation of Fidesz with zsidó, the Hungarian for "Jew" or "Jewish"). But from the moment that Orbán and company were not on the bandwagon, and had found their way into the little black book, nothing was off-limits—and in one fell swoop Fidesz was an object of opprobrium in the Hungarian media. From then on, Orbán and his people were lumped in with other adversaries, and the same rules applied to them as applied to their erstwhile opponents.

Soros's revenge blasted Fidesz.

At the same time, Orbán and his team learned that the accusation of anti-Semitism is a symptom. When the accusation rears its head, the friend–foe recognition system is activated, and the matter is closed. This is the harshest accusation imaginable. It is unthinkable about them, and yet it is the allegation; and when the accusation of anti-Semitism is made against you there is nothing you can do.

Let us not forget that we are talking about Hungary. In the Second World War Hungary was on the side of the Germans. And in a country that in the Second World War played a role in the Holocaust—albeit a supporting role to the Germans—the accusation of anti-Semitism is instantly lethal.

When accusations of anti-Semitism appeared, it became clear to everyone on both sides that this story would not end in rapprochement.

....

On the night of the second round of the 1994 general election, a messenger arrived at Fidesz headquarters. A fashion photographer who had made his fortune in America approached Orbán with the news that everything had been decided: there would be an MSZP-SZDSZ government. The offer was for Fidesz to join the government, with one ministerial portfolio and two state secretariats. To this Orbán said: "No way!" He sent the messenger away with a flea in his ear.

This idea was certainly not the brainchild of the MSZP leader Gyula Horn, nor did the generous offer come from the SZDSZ. The SZDSZ needed to be grateful, they had all the support they could ask for from everyone—including from US ambassadors and Soros. The SZDSZ had no problem in reaching an agreement with the post-communists in terms of family ties either, because they came from the same place. So their alliance with the MSZP was justifiable in terms of politics of power (gratitude) and culture (Bolshevik roots). But why would Fidesz have been needed?

Fidesz suspected that Soros had a hand in this, and that it was something he had decreed. The offer was not justified by the election results: Fidesz had barely won enough seats to get into Parliament, and together the MSZP and the SZDSZ had a two-thirds majority. And yet they made an offer to Fidesz. But it was justified by something else: the consideration that in the long term the only way to keep Orbán and his team under control was to drag them into government. Better safe than sorry: "If we pull them in, they're already in our pocket, and in government they'll certainly do something which will give us leverage over Orbán later." And the icing on the cake was that an MSZP-SZDSZ-Fidesz government would be formed so that the mistakes made by the MDF could be corrected by this great democratic conglomerate.

Orbán's refusal was interpreted as disobedience. Orbán was adamant, however.

. . . .

In 1994 Orbán lost.

Two years earlier it looked as if Fidesz would be forming the next government, and Orbán would become Prime Minister. That did not happen. Over the course of eighteen months, Fidesz's support had fallen from forty percent to seven percent. The young, talented Orbán, who had previously been lionized by the press, had become the Devil himself, whose accession to power should be feared, because he was a dictator, because he was anti-Semitic — and also because he no longer even looked trustworthy.

Soros sat back and smiled. In 1994 it seemed to him that the victory of the MSZP-SZDSZ coalition had put things on track. He saw this as a personal victory. Everything was in order in the province called Hungary. What was more, his plans for the region were shaping up nicely.

He had set up his Moscow branch back in 1987. Although, a few years later, Moscow rejected Soros's crisis management recipe, Boris Yeltsin exempted Soros's organizations from paying taxes, duties, and fees. So Soros had a foothold in Moscow, and in almost the whole of the post-Soviet space. After the break-up of the Soviet Union, branch organizations opened in the Baltic states, Georgia and the "-stans." Soros's organizations supported cultural efforts in Albania and financed state-building in Macedonia and Belarus. Soros had foundations in Bulgaria, Yugoslavia, and Romania. And, of course, he had built strong bridge-heads in Poland and Czechoslovakia, through his support for civil society.

There were flashes here and there: some provinces were in disarray, and there was resistance on one issue or another. But in essence things were fine. By the early 1990s, Soros the philanthropic billionaire had become a stateless statesman, and the Soviet empire had become the Soros empire.

Although Orbán had lost, he also won. Orbán had been able to stand up to Soros. The political movement he led had retained its autonomy and was able to govern itself. And this self-reliant, independent movement had always been, and remained, the essence and touchstone of anti-communism and national sovereignty.

A Hot Tin Roof

1995

Times were changing. Éva was no longer running a Trabant, but was running Soros's foundation in Hungary. She had been the boss there for some time now, and would remain so until 2001.

Éva Bakonyi had worked for a business support foundation since the early 1990s, and was said to have done a very good job. She was skilled not in the world of intellectual ballyhoo, but in business. Soros was unhappy with the Hungarian foundation: it was chaotic, nothing was right, matters had been settled on the basis of friendship, and he wanted change. This is why he put Éva in charge.

She ran the shop while her partner, Gábor Horn, coordinated Soros's education development program. By 1995, as things were already on track, Bálint Magyar—one of the leaders of the SZDSZ—had managed to get Soros to support two policy programs: education and health care. The big issues were in place, so why not smaller issues? Soros liked the idea very much, as it fitted in with his concept of the open society.

Gábor Horn was allowed to spend one and a half billion forints a year on education, and was given a free hand. It was an incredible amount of money. Soros was a state within the state.

....

So Soros had established himself in Hungary. After the new government came to power, he arranged for his university (CEU) to get accreditation. Fidesz saw this as gaining an advantage through a violation of the law. It was

CEU's original sin that someone was able to do something (whether good or bad) simply because they had enough money. Orbán and his team saw that the state had been tricked into approving CEU. Furthermore, the Minister of Education in this new government was Gábor Fodor, Orbán's former roommate, who left Fidesz in 1993 to join the SZDSZ. Fodor was seen as giving Soros a privileged position, personally granting accreditation so that Soros's university could operate with the appearance of abiding by the rules. This was a frog that Fidesz could not swallow.

Soros also arranged for Bill Gates to attend the launch of Windows 95 in Budapest. On a beautiful sunny morning at the Karinthy Frigyes Bilingual High School, two of the world's richest men—Soros and Gates—had a nice chat with Hungarian students. Their meeting was organized by Gábor Horn.

Horn was also the man Soros called on when he wanted to turn his personal ambitions into reality. "Gábor, I'd like to ask you for something. I'd like to build a school in Almádi." In the Hungarian town of Balatonalmádi there lived an old lady who had given refuge to Soros's mother during the Second World War. When she turned eighty, Soros asked her what she would like, and she asked him for a school. And the school was built. Gábor Horn, Soros's man, built from scratch what is probably the most beautiful school in the country, with a view of Lake Balaton from every window. The interesting thing is that later, in an interview with a Hungarian weekly in around 2005, Soros said that unfortunately—much to his disappointment—the lady in question, Elza Brandeisz (in whose honor a tree was planted at the Yad Vashem Remembrance Center in Jerusalem when she was made one of the "Righteous among the Nations" by the state of Israel), was a reader of the conservative daily *Magyar Nemzet* ("Hungarian Nation"). What was more, this formerly respectable, decent woman was now expressing stridently anti-Roma opinions; and obviously all this was only possible because the right-wing

Magyar Nemzet was inciting hatred of the Roma. The newspaper then published an angry piece criticizing Soros, but this was an exceptional occurrence: in the second half of the 1990s there was no trace of similar pieces in either the Hungarian or the Western press.

Then, in the mid-1990s, Soros called Gábor Horn to ask if he could arrange some kind of summer job for his children. They had worked every summer since they were fourteen, because their father did not want them to be spoiled, and Soros thought it would be good for them to do something in Hungary that summer. Horn asked, "What kind of work?" Soros replied, "The shittier the better!"

It was as if Soros had—wittingly or unwittingly—formulated his personal philosophy.

....

Members of the SZDSZ leadership regularly went to Soros for an audience. They even went to New York if necessary. When, in the mid-1990s, Gábor Horn visited him and his family in America, Soros said that he could stay in his mother's apartment (Soros's mother had died shortly before Horn's visit). It was a modestly sized apartment on 40th Street in midtown Manhattan. When Horn walked into the apartment, he felt exactly as if he were at his grandmother's: the same furniture, the same "geriatric aroma." It was exactly as if he were visiting his own grandmother in Budapest's District XIII. The way that Soros's mother had lived in the heart of New York was just as she would have if she were on Pozsonyi Road, Budapest. By contrast, Soros's residence revealed nothing about who Soros was or where he came from: impersonal bourgeois luxury; not even any Hungarian books. Soros's home could have been anywhere.

....

Just as Soros could have been living anywhere, so he could have been born anywhere. According to his Hungarian friends, Soros is an emotionally damaged man. He had no tearful nostalgia for anything—including Hungary.

Once, back in the late 1980s, when Soros was bringing his wife to Budapest, he asked the taxi driver to turn off at the street where he used to live before the war. The taxi driver thought that they would get out of the car, and that maybe Soros would stroke the front railings. But nothing of the sort happened: Soros pointed out the building from the car, and they drove on.

No one remembers Soros doing anything like having a beer with someone just because he felt like it. He did not have any real friendships with his people in Hungary, giving the impression of someone with no emotions. He spoke to everyone in a measured and purposeful way. He had business, but not emotions. "I cannot imagine how he could tell someone he loved them! I don't think he could—and he had a couple of wives," his former secretary said of him.

Apart from making money, perhaps the only thing that still fired him up was chess(!), in which he displayed a passionate interest. Interestingly enough, his favorite chess partner was Sándor Demján: a leading businessman in the late-Kádár world, who became Orbán's favorite partner in the Hungarian card game *Ulti*. While chess is all about checkmate, Ulti is all about winning the final trick.

The only thing he could appreciate was advancement and development in material terms. When his former secretary János Betlen went to meet him at Budapest's Ferihegy airport, he borrowed a large Mazda from a friend. Soros looked at János with approval: he had not expected such a breakthrough from a man in a sweater and a Trabant.

....

Back then, Orbán drove a 1.6-liter Opel Corsa and did not feel successful. He had not yet achieved what he wanted to achieve in his profession, in politics.

He had to rethink a number of things, how to proceed, what he needed to do differently, and what he had learned from his failures. In short, he had to roll up his sleeves.

1998

An eventful year. There was war in Kosovo. Helmut Kohl was defeated in the German election, and stepped down after sixteen years in power. France won the World Cup final against Brazil. Larry Page and Sergey Brin founded Google. Hungarian TV broadcast the first episode of the soap opera *Barátok közt* ("Among Friends"), which would run for almost twenty-five years. Budapest was the scene of bloody gangland killings. Emir Kusturica's romantic black comedy *Black Cat, White Cat* and Guy Ritchie's *Lock, Stock and Two Smoking Barrels* premiered in cinemas. Hungary's largest commercial radio station, Sláger Rádió, was launched. Atop of the charts were Baby Sisters' *Hoppá!!!*, TNT's *Bumm*, and *Vétkezz velem!*, performed by V-Tech.

In Hungary, Orbán would, after all, be Number One. Thirty-four years old when he won the election, but already thirty-five when he was sworn in as Prime Minister, Orbán was the youngest government leader in Europe. He had won a stunning victory, ploughing up the country, winning Hungary village by village.

At that time, general elections in Hungary were held in two rounds. After the first round the post-communists led Fidesz by a hair's breadth. Then the overbearing former communist policeman Gyula Horn agreed to a head-to-head TV debate with Orbán — and lost. The post-communists lost the election as well.

Gyula Horn was the epitome of the superannuated communist world. He embodied everything that Fidesz was determined to defeat and leave behind. But that world was a powerful one: defeating him was a feat equivalent to the fourteen-year-old Krisztina Egerszegi winning a gold medal for Hungary at the 1988 Olympics ahead of two burly East Germans, a worldwide sensation.

....

Word of this spread all the way to New York. From America,

at that time, it was impossible to know what Orbán's government would look like and what it would do. Bill Clinton would invite Orbán to the White House. A dinner was held at which Orbán was able to tell members of the American liberal elite what the state of play in Hungary was. The organizer of this dinner was a Hungarian woman called Kati Marton, who — significantly — was the wife of the US special envoy to the Balkans, Richard Holbrooke, and one of the Soros empire's leading intellectual figures in New York. This was the third time Orbán and Soros had met; the task was to enter the lion's den and come out alive.

All the big hitters of the liberal Western world were at the dinner. Elie Wiesel was there; he had announced that, because of the Holocaust, he would not speak Hungarian — although he at least understood the language.* UN Secretary-General Kofi Annan was there — and, of course, Soros. It was here that Orbán discovered Soros's mastery of an interesting game: although his mother tongue was Hungarian, when he was talking to Hungarians and things went in what he saw as an unfavorable direction — in other words, whenever he thought it useful — he would simply "forget" his Hungarian. Thus the conversation would run into the sand. He did not confront opposing opinions, but would slip out of the whole thing, like an eel. He would pretend not to know what the other person was talking about, and that was the end of it.

Kati Marton had done Orbán and his team a favor by inviting them to dinner. Orbán was given the opportunity to draw a positive starting line: "There's a new Hungarian government, this is what we look like, we want this, we're going in this direction, and we can develop a positive relationship with the American liberal elite."

Orbán's contribution was electrifying. He went through every issue that could later be raised as a criticism. He

---

* A Nobel Peace Prize-winning author, he grew up in Romania and Hungary, speaking Yiddish, German, Romanian, and Hungarian.

talked about Russia, regional policy, the economy, the Roma situation, and the issue of Hungarians beyond the country's borders. On the Hungarian side, the aim was to clear the landmines before they exploded. And what were the American mines? That was quite clear. There followed a very serious exchange of ideas at the table: about philosophical issues, about the world, about the "big picture."

That evening Soros was not hostile, confrontational, or even nitpicking. In any case, it is typical of him that he likes to remain silent—and he can be very attentive. Soros was silent and he listened very attentively.

That evening nothing was asked of Orbán, nothing was offered him, and he was not even threatened. Orbán emerged from the lion's den in one piece.

....

Then, as a result of Orbán's governance, this favorable American tailwind disappeared. After the New York meeting in 1998 hopes were high, but they evaporated. Bush junior won in 2000, the Democrats were out, and the Republicans were in. Orbán had quite good relations with the latter—until it became clear that we were not going to buy their planes. After the Gripen affair Orbán was hit by a tsunami of anger and hatred; and the problem was not just that Lockheed Martin had missed out on a big payday.

America was humiliatingly hostile. Orbán has said that if we had taken it personally we would have been humiliated. American diplomacy is based on the cheap notepaper principle: they hand you a piece of paper with their conditions written on it, and they expect you to accept them. Those who dictate the ground rules are the hegemon, and the yes-men are those who accept those rules without question.

For Orbán, however, that was enough reason to reject them. Orbán was not—and never has been—a yes-man. At the time, given the consequences, this may have been stupid or a downright mistake; but sovereignty mattered to him more than anything else.

A staff member from the US Embassy appeared in the office of one of the Hungarian prime minister's senior advisers. He began shouting, demanding to know what had gotten into the Hungarians. No one should imagine that it mattered to them whether Orbán would buy some Gripen fighter jets from Sweden instead of F-16s from the US. Obviously that would have been nice, but in America they did not care about that; the main problem was that this created a precedent, and they would not stand for it.

....

That was what one could call the personal aspect of the hostility. But there was also an ideological aspect, the awe-inspiring practice of soft power: a devious action plan to assert American interests through NGOs, foundations, civil society organizations, and the media. That was the goal, and the Americans saw that it could be achieved through Soros.

And Soros gave the order: "We must all take the right track. If so far our strategy has been to have no strategy, now our strategy is to have a strategy."

CEU had to be set on the right track. The moment had come to bring to life the monster which the designer himself had created, and which would thus acquire its true meaning—and, to avoid any misunderstanding, this was not as a university or as talent management. The civil society organizations had to be set on the right track: they had to raise Cain and keep the government under pressure. The media had to be set on the right track. The Gripen affair had provided a good opportunity to accuse Orbán of being anti-American—and anyone who is anti-American is considered to be opposed to the free world, and, therefore, to be building a dictatorship. Then came the anti-Semitism accusation, and the friend–foe recognition system was activated again. Fidesz was anti-Semitic because it provided a second home for members of the MDF and the Smallholders Party: they were anti-Semitic, so Fidesz must also be anti-Semitic.

From a strategic point of view the whole Gripen affair was good for Soros, enabling him to pigeonhole Fidesz and exclude it from polite society. So he killed two birds with one stone: he blacklisted it, and created opposition to it that would be useful in the 2002 election campaign. And it would be pointless to tell the Hungarian people that they must be sovereign and strong-willed, because they were dependent on the American world in a thousand ways.

In America, too, there was a slew of derogatory writings which had been dictated verbatim from Hungary. The SZDSZ took the anti-Semitic card to New York, and then they said: "Here's what the world thinks of you!" Bálint Magyar and his circle enjoyed great prestige in the West, and for them exporting this narrative was perfectly natural. Even the US-based Hungarian-born political scientist Charles Gati was hyping up Orbán's alleged anti-Semitism, and it resonated in America.

When an article attacking the Hungarian government appeared in the US magazine *Foreign Affairs*, Orbán's foreign affairs adviser approached the author and asked her if she had ever been to Hungary. The answer was no. Had she ever met any Hungarians? No, she had not. Did she speak Hungarian? No, she did not. Had she read any Hungarian texts? No, she had not. It was a very unpleasant confrontation for her, and after that she never wrote anything about Hungarians. But Orbán and his team did not have the resources to confront everyone personally and tell the American world that these were just partisan opinions. And perhaps they did not have enough bandwidth for it.

With the purchase of those planes, Orbán wanted to send a signal to America that there was no room for the attitude of just coming here and making demands (nor did he allow missiles to be stationed on Hungary's southern border). But the hegemon's signal in response was that this was something you could not do.

The irritations over his disobedience ("What does Orbán think he's doing?") were clothed by the hegemon in anti-Semitic garb—and in this a major role was played by Soros. Three years after Orbán took office, all the governmental, diplomatic, intelligence, and financial initiatives aimed at overthrowing the Hungarian government ran in parallel with destabilization attempts cloaked in Soros-backed accusations of anti-Semitism. So between 1998 and 2002 it was very clear that Soros was funding causes and people who were opponents of the government that Orbán had set up.

. . . .

America's main competitive advantage over everyone else was that it recognized the importance of soft power, built a network for it, and operated it systematically—with more or less the same recipe everywhere. And this is why Soros was useful to America. This does not necessarily mean that Soros was the same as America, but on any particular issue there was a high probability that he would be the same. There was a productive synergy between America and Soros. America used Soros, and, whenever he could, Soros used America—for profit.

But America has two faces. Soros is the sworn enemy of Republican America. He has never hidden his antipathy towards the America of George W. Bush or Donald Trump. He has done much to make the world see the Republican President George W. Bush as a sinister southern savage in the fight against terrorism, and Trump as a chump—a boor, whose presidency must be sabotaged at all costs. In 2018 he straightforwardly claimed that Donald Trump's presidency was a threat to the whole world. Through organizations such as Human Rights Watch, America Coming Together, and America Votes, he has instigated massive barrages of criticism against Republican-led US policy in the fight against terrorism, on racism, on the treatment of illegal migrants, and on drug-related legislation. On the other hand, in almost every way—including as a mega-donor—he has helped and supported pro-Democrat goals, programs, and individuals in America. This is a long list, which includes Barack Obama. He has openly claimed to have discovered Obama and supported his campaign. But during his presidency Soros was disappointed that he was not being listened to (in 2010, after he gave Obama a list of things he should do, the latter stopped seeking him out). But he has developed a particularly warm and close relationship with the Clintons, who share his worldview. How could it be otherwise?

In the name of a common worldview, Soros has swallowed the Left whole. His place is with drug addicts, transsexuals, those struggling with mental problems, sex workers, pro-abortionists, euthanasia advocates, anti-gun and race activists, climate radicals, and illegal immigrants.

His position is that reducing the harm to those suffering from addiction is a human right, and that, in a just society, drug policy rests on the foundation of science, compassion, health, and human rights. In decriminalizing marijuana, his lead is being followed not only by some US states, but also by many European countries (Germany, Portugal, Belgium, the Netherlands). In 2014 Forbes named him America's greatest drug reformer, fighting—alongside the presidents of Brazil, Guatemala, and Uruguay—to end the "senseless and socially damaging" war on drugs.

Soros is a champion of support for migration and is an implacable enemy of borders, walls, and fences. In Soros's eyes another enemy is national culture, and cancel culture is a means of attacking national culture—especially if that national culture is a white, "heteronormative," and male-dominated culture. Black Lives Matter: this is what Soros offers instead as a new tool for societal disruption.

But the form of soft power thought to be most easily exportable has become gender.

The consideration underlying this was that at some point the Holocaust would no longer be a sustainable mainstream ideology, and something else would have to replace it. Interestingly enough, the Holocaust was not even a leading issue until the 1960s; then suddenly some people took it up, and the accusation of anti-Semitism became the highest trump card—eventually even being used against Orbán. In the hands of the soft-power wizards, the Holocaust was also a way to paper over the communist/anti-communist dichotomy; and players in the Western world were also involved in this. So the word was that the dichotomy was not to be dealt with, because doing so was not at all in the Left's interest. But it was also clear that sooner or later the Holocaust would be overshadowed by something else, and that there would be a theme that would displace it. And what was that theme? Gender! And who caused the displacement? Soros! And here again, it was no accident that there was a confrontation between Orbán and Soros. There is Orbán, who, when talking about the family, says that a father is a man, a mother is a woman, and our children must be left alone. And then there is Soros, who does the same thing with gender as he does with philanthropy or any other issue: "After all, everyone is human, so why shouldn't a family be this, that, or something else? Love is love. Anyone can love anyone, and that's a good thing. And anyone who goes against this is doing evil to people or to humanity, so he can't be anything but evil. Because he who opposes good is evil." Therefore anyone who comes up with a child protection law and gives priority to the traditional family model will be the Devil. This looks like a winning game. From Orbán's point of view, however, the Child Protection Act is a warning signal, saying, "Pay attention, use your heads! All this permissive talk is leading us into the sheep pen, and in fact it's all being paid for and being organized by none other than Soros."

As long as soft power was blue jeans, Coca-Cola, McDonald's, and *Playboy*, it was a hit. Everyone was in love with America. After gender came into the picture, it has seemed like a harder sell. It is certainly not a secondary battlefront, and it is also certain that Soros is doing everything he can, through his organizational network, to make this theme dominate the world. Yet it feels as if America is no longer as sexy as it once was.

....

The shift in Soviet political life came in the 1970s or there-
abouts, when they stopped worrying about soft power politics.
Brezhnev was so sure of himself, things were going so well,
and America was in such trouble (Vietnam, Watergate) that
they gave up on it. And then *Rocky, Rambo,* and *Red Heat*
showed everyone that if you bet on soft power, you could
win everything. To this day, the Russians have no soft power
policy, and it is no wonder they get bad press in the Western
world. It is as if they have forgotten the old political wisdom
that if you do not point out the evil one, then you will be
pointed out as the evil one. Today Putin is the evil one, who
is also doing evil, and who has no place in our civilization.

The Chinese are beginning to discover what soft power
is about. It is dawning on them, and there is a reason why
the hegemon is angry. Legend has it that, as a child, Xi
Jinping was working in a mountain village when he got his
hands on a copy of Goethe's *Faust,* and loved it so much
that he learned it by heart. Faust is the only lens through
which Western analysts can try to see into the mind of one
of the world's most powerful men. But what is Xi's *Faust*
about? Is it that China will never be subjugated? Is it that
his economic philosophy is Faustian? (Faust, when he wants
to reclaim fertile land from the sea, is complicit in an act
of cruelty.) Is the new artificial man, *Homunculus,* being
created in Chinese alchemists' workshops? Is human history
being driven forward by machination and intrigue? Or is it
simply—as one internet meme aptly puts it—that "God
created the world, but everything else is made in China"?

The idea that we Hungarians should engage in soft power,
or that we ourselves should embody soft power, was con-
ceptually out of the question. A province should be seen
and not heard.

....

As we know, Orbán lost the 2002 elections. Then he lost
again in 2006.

1 8 1 8

....

This year saw the publication of the novel that would make Mary Shelley's career: *Frankenstein; or, the Modern Prometheus.* When she wrote it she was only nineteen. The book's storyline was inspired by a vision in which Mary saw the pale student of an ungodly science kneeling beside a creature of his own creation. The creature is capable of development, learning from the behavior of others and acquiring scientific knowledge, but is also capable of evil deeds. Its creator is called Victor because Mary Shelley was greatly influenced by John Milton's *Paradise Lost,* in which Milton frequently refers to God as "the Victor." And indeed Mary Shelley portrays Victor as playing God, and creating life: "I doubted at first whether I should attempt the creation of a being like myself . . . but my imagination was too much exalted by my first success to permit me to doubt of my ability to give life to an animal as complex and wonderful as man." But the dream was shattered, and the creature became a true monster, which provoked disgust and horror in its creator: "His limbs were in proportion, and I had selected his features as beautiful. Beautiful! — Great God! His yellow skin scarcely covered the work of muscles and arteries beneath; his hair was of a lustrous black, and flowing; his teeth of a pearly whiteness; but these luxuriances only formed a more horrid contrast with his watery eyes, that seemed almost of the same colour as the dun white sockets in which they were set, his shrivelled complexion and straight black lips." He "became a thing such as even Dante could not have conceived," and most of all he resembled the Satan of *Paradise Lost,* threatening to "glut the maw of death."

Perhaps one of the most interesting consequences of all this is that, as a result of countless reworkings, mass culture has come to confuse the creator with his creation. It is widely believed that Frankenstein is the name of the monster, when it is merely the surname of Victor, the creature's creator. And the creature is deliberately left unnamed:

sometimes he is called a "creature," "being," "devil," "daemon," or "wretch." The horror adaptations have also reduced the philosophical depth of the work: Frankenstein's creation becomes a soulless zombie, whereas the original story was about the problem of ostracism, which should awaken feelings of pity in any person of good conscience.

....

But what is the *modus operandi* of this creature—who is greater than his creator, and who survives him?

As we have seen, there is a philosopher with a god complex, with messianic views, and a billionaire to boot. (The only year in which he recorded a loss was 1981, and he later said that he had to ask himself who was more important, himself or the creature he had created; and he voted for himself—he won and the Fund lost.) His money and influence make him one of the most powerful men in the world, and certainly one of the most powerful philosophers. His aim, however, is not to understand the world, but to change it. So the philosopher has political goals.

Soros is the antithesis of the modern Right. Entire generations are now thinking in the liberal "Esperanto" created by Soros. After Marx he is without doubt the most directly influential philosopher of all time. Over the course of many decades this philanthropic philosopher has built a power factory of global proportions. His method is not to enter politics openly (not to take a political role, not to contest elections, not to be seen), but to intervene from outside in order to create chaos. Either he intervenes from the outset, where instability already exists, or he intervenes in order to create instability. These are the circumstances that create the conditions for his primary political activity: speculation. He has no moral scruples, he will misuse anyone, he is the enemy of stability—that value considered to be of crucial importance for societal peace.

When its origins are external, intervention is a breach of sovereignty. In this event, how things should be is not determined by the will of those within the state in question, and the direction that things should take is not decided by citizens in their own country: it is decided from outside, by removing sovereign will. The creature brought to life by Soros is therefore not only destroying the cement of societal peace and stability, but also attacking sovereignty—which is seen as the essence of self-determination. The Soros empire is a covert structure that attacks sovereignty.

At the same time, it is insensitive to the kind of society it is destroying, and in which it is creating political chaos. It has invested billions of dollars and enormous political energies in preventing Brexit, in financing political action groups opposed to Trump, and in supporting color revolutions or attempts at them (Georgia, the Maldives, Ukraine, Belarus, Lebanon, Tunisia, Egypt, Syria). Everywhere the result is chaos, and the consignment bearing an American airmail stamp that is dropped off is inflatable democracy— with hand pump included.

Its social agenda is therefore "blank." It can target not only any political regime, but any political system—including democracy itself. The Soros empire is the enemy of the values on which democracy is based. Soros says that he has enough money to be unconstrained by any rules of play, and similarly has enough money to simply change those rules he does not like. He is not concerned with the principle of the will of the majority, voter empowerment, oversight, accountability, or popular sovereignty. He is "blank," and impervious to democratic principles.

As well as being blank, the Soros empire is also—per-haps surprisingly, at first sight—indifferent to liberal prin-ciples. While it styles itself as championing all the great principles that the spirit of the age demands because they are unquestionably positive (a just, open society; trans-parency; fundamental human rights; the rule of law), in reality the Soros empire does not do battle in a transparent way. The Soros network operates through multiple overlap-ping personnel teams, in unclear ways, and using opaque financial strategies and indirect methods (it is ironic that Soros named one of his institutes "Transparency International"). Or look at a favorite liberal *topos*: the issue of minority rights. In North Macedonia, for example, Soros stood for the rights of the Albanian minority, while in prewar Ukraine he supported a regime that opposed minority rights. So it is not the rights of minorities that matter, but the potential for disruption. This is quite aside from the fact that the fundamental value of liberal and democratic societies is the concept of the rule of law, according to which the law applies equally to everyone. Soros, however, considers himself and his institutions to be above the law: although all universities in Hungary are subject to the same laws, CEU—he argued—could not be subject to those laws. The Soros empire is therefore neither democratic nor liberal, but merely blank—or, worse, totalitarian.

Soros has said that his aim is to open up closed societies; and, indeed, he has been adept at finding the weaknesses in the "closed societies" he targets, and opening them up. And so he occupies their justice systems and prosecutors' offices, because this provides an excellent platform from which to protect his own people and to take down the network's political opponents—as happened in Romania, for example. And so he orchestrates ethnic conflicts, as he has done in Albania or North Macedonia, because internal disorder can be used to destabilize governments and break down sovereign will. And so he demands economic reforms and imposes forced privatization, because this is the way to gain influence in the life and governments of sovereign economies—as shown by the examples of Poland and Ukraine. And he has used all possible means to support "color revolutions" against "oppression," in order to create confusion and then overthrow autonomous regimes with external support and violence. His avowed aim, therefore, is to promote openness and freedom by dismantling what he sees as totalitarian, closed societies. But in reality, the Soros empire is itself totalitarian. In order to achieve its goals, it extends its reach into all areas of life:

from school milk programs to funding for periodicals, from lawfare against political opponents to openly influencing political decision-making. The Soros empire looks for structural locations for intervention. It seeks to gain cultural power. Higher education, mass media, the production, interpretation, and control of news, the "democratization" of science, and the domination of publishing, art, and the entertainment and film industries are all seen by it as strategic areas. It maintains rating and classifying organizations—which can rate, but cannot be rated themselves (Amnesty International, Freedom House, the Helsinki Committees, Transparency International). Its aim is to dismantle "closed" identities everywhere: to "delegitimize" the traditional notion of the family, by promoting LGBTQ rights; to "delegitimize" nations, by promoting migration, multiculturalism, and supranational organizations and solutions; to "delegitimize" the meaning of life, by promoting euthanasia, abortion, and the legalization of recreational drug use. It openly supports progressive causes in order to engender social disorder, and it promotes rebellious opposition to "delegitimized" power—from non-violent resistance to color revolutions.

Soros is also full-on in the means he uses to exert political pressure. He builds strongholds and bridgeheads around the world. He incites chaos and confusion to maximize profits. He has raised a formidable army of intellectuals, media professionals, and civil society activists. The creature is indeed surpassing its creator's original conception, through a vast network of foundations, the coordinated work of NGOs, the mobilization of human rights organizations, and thousands upon thousands of Soros troops. It is not the creator but the creature that seizes the state, occupies the front line in political life, seeks to gain overt or covert influence, finances opposition organizations, imprisons "corrupt" members of ruling political elites, and creates political chaos, threatening social order and the security of ordinary people.

A common feature of Soros's political involvement is that he has encouraged street protests, civil society movements, and progressive media everywhere. His organizations have trained activists, instructed them in "street fighting," and organized protest movements. Soros has financed such processes in Ukraine (the infamous "Orange Revolution"), Slovakia (against Mečiar), and the former Yugoslavia (against Milošević).

It is interesting to imagine what it would be like if you were to turn up the volume of what you say by, perhaps, one hundred thousand. You could not even count the number of countries in which a choir was singing instead of you. "But," ask sincere humanities graduates, "what's wrong with that, if you mean well?" The whole Soros thesis is based on the assumption that the prime mover himself remains invisible. Since he does not have to justify himself, he cannot be delegitimized. The delegitimization that targets the existing establishment is not carried out by Soros himself, but by the network he funds. Soros does not believe in votes and mandates, but solely and exclusively in money.

Soros is very proud that he is at the same level as the professors who sit on his boards of trustees, but it is not as if he runs the whole world. He has all these eminent professors sitting on his boards of trustees saying all manner of wild things — for example, that it is good that there are restrictions on immigrants entering America legally, but it is not good for there to be restrictions on immigrants entering illegally! Or that, in the final analysis, it is good to say that women can give birth, but it is not good to say that men cannot give birth! Soros is very proud that he sits at the top of this, but in fact he has used this money to buy his way in at the same level as the professors and statesmen. He is a little like Kanye West: highly successful, almost a genius at what he does, but a narcissist who is intoxicated with megalomaniac fantasies. He has written a book about himself (*Soros on Soros: Staying Ahead of the Curve*), and in interviews he has made no secret of his opinion of his own importance as a genius for whom the world has been waiting.

The political philanthropy pursued by Soros is also about money opening doors—and there is money to open any door. Soros's political philanthropy is based on a profoundly pessimistic political anthropology. According to Soros, man is "empty": not driven by higher ideals, and not interested in truth. As such, a human being is *nihil*. Therefore he or she is a blank page, on which anything can be written. The money exists with which anyone can be bought. The "blank" Soros no doubt savors the irony: for is there anything more ironic than the fact that Soros's payroll is replete with liberal intellectuals who pride themselves on their moral fiber and boast of their autonomy?

So Soros buys everything and everyone he can. And anyone he does not buy, he pushes aside with the force of a totalitarian empire, with its network extending to all areas of life. He even pushes aside democratically elected leaders who are not strong or canny enough to resist.

In a democracy, power comes from the ballot box. A large plurality of votes gives great strength. Sometimes, even in a democracy, someone can be so strong that it costs too much to overthrow them, and—beyond a certain point—it is simply not worth it for the billionaire speculator. From this point of view, it would also be worth considering the question of why Europe has so many coalition governments—in other words, governments dependent on compromises, and therefore weak.

Orbán had to confront this creature, the mighty Soros empire, and Soros avoided Orbán like a cat recoiling from a hot tin roof.

....

Orbán also avoided Soros. This was the case even though Soros repeatedly offered to meet with Orbán after 1998. But Orbán avoided such encounters. He did not want Soros to ask or offer anything, and avoided meeting with him because he knew that they were not in the same weight division. He also avoided it as a challenge and a task that he would have to complete at some point if he was serious about governing this country.

In 1998 Orbán sought out the poet Sándor Csoóri. Having won the election that year, he felt it was time to set a national cultural policy, and wanted advice on how to go about it. All Csoóri said was that the subject was not worth talking about seriously as long as Soros was giving more money to culture and funding more people than the government was. "When you change that, Viktor, then we can talk about it." Orbán thought that these were wise words.

2010

In 2010 Orbán instigated a revolution in the polling booths. He was able to form a government for the second time, and he could do so with a commanding two-thirds majority. But for this, he had had to endure eight years in opposition, with the Soros-backed forces returning to government in 2002. In 2002, Soros was made an honorary citizen of Budapest (receiving an 18-carat gold medal, an inch in diameter, with the inscription *Civis Honoris Causa Budapestini*—"those who do not appreciate the small things in life do not deserve the big things"), and in 2004 he was awarded the Grand Cross of the Hungarian Order of Merit, civil division. His virtues were being recognized, and CEU was flourishing. Meanwhile the economic crisis was deepening, and in 2008 Soros targeted OTP again.

In 2010, however, Orbán won. They had not met for twelve years, but finally they met again—and once more when Orbán was forming a government. Back then they did not know that it would be their final meeting.

Soros knocked on Orbán's door after the red mud industrial disaster.* His right-hand man at the time, Kálmán Mizsei, had sent the message that Soros would be happy to meet. Orbán invited him for a coffee in the Parliament building, and while he was there asked him to support the victims of the red mud disaster (Soros did, generously giving a million dollars). But this was not why Soros came. He came to Orbán because he wanted to continue his projects for the Roma in Hungary and wanted to talk about them. Orbán thought this was a very good idea; in any case he wanted to do a lot of things, and so there was a lot to talk about. Orbán then told Soros that he grew up in a small

---

* An industrial accident at a caustic waste reservoir at the Ajkai Timföldgyár alumina plant in western Hungary, resulting in the release of one million cubic meters (thirty-five million cubic feet) of liquid waste, or "red mud," flooding nearby settlements. Ten people died, and hundreds were injured.

village where there were always one or two gypsy families, that he knew them, that he had gypsy classmates and had gotten on well with them. "So in Hungarian politics I am the one who knows the most about gypsy issues." In reply, Soros said that in fact he—the New York billionaire—was the one who knew most about them! So Soros is not only a very clever Hungarian, but he also has a sense of humor. It was then agreed that the Roma programs would continue—or, more precisely, that Orbán would not stop them. He could easily have done so: Soros's ideas about the meaning of the Roma issue were very different from those of Orbán. He financed Roma organizations that worked to create a Roma identity that was emotionally and deliberately opposed to any Hungarian ethnic identity. In contrast, Orbán was thinking in terms of integrationism and strengthening national identity. In other words, for him a Roma person is Hungarian; meanwhile, for Soros, in political terms, the whole point is for the Roma to be organized on an ethnic basis against the majority Hungarian ethnicity.

Despite that agreement, the conflict over the Roma issue had always been there under the surface. In 2012, when Zoltán Balog became Minister for Human Capacities, he said that social inclusion needed to actively involve the minority population, and that the Roma issue was ultimately a Hungarian issue. On the issue of social inclusion, there had to be a confrontation with Soros, even if this could not be made public. Soros and his people tried to exert pressure from both the inside and the outside. It was rumored that Soros wanted to create an autonomous Roma region in Northern Hungary, which would have meant weakening the central state through the orchestration of ethnic conflicts. But Hungary did not become North Macedonia.* Soros also tried to exert external pressure: in 2013, one of the Orbán government's greatest feats of arms came when it prevented the EU from outsourcing Roma policy to Soros.

---

* Until 1991 the Socialist Republic of Macedonia, part of Yugoslavia.

In Brussels they claimed that they were the ones with the knowledge to solve the problem.

And then all this kicking and punching under the surface of the water on the Roma issue was immediately taken off the agenda by the migration crisis that erupted in 2015.

....

If Orbán is in government, then Soros at the very least will be fortifying and bankrolling the opposition—under the surface, of course. This was always as natural to him as breathing. Then came "deep breathing" exercises: attacks through the press. It is still possible to defend oneself somehow against the accusation of denying democracy: elections are held, anyone can stand, and the people decide, thank you very much! One can also defend oneself against accusations related to economic performance, because one can point to the economic situation in the country that one had to start out from, and then point to the direction the country is heading in; so the facts protect one to some extent. Then, of course, there is the accusation of corruption: it is difficult to prove corruption, but it is easier to accuse anyone of it. But to prove that an accusation is false, that there was no corruption, is virtually impossible. The anti-Semitism accusation, like the latter, is also not a factual accusation: there are no facts; and if there are none, there is no factual language you can use to defend against it. There is therefore no defense. Not even the fact that you have done a list of things to curb anti-Semitism is a defense—because, after all, you have not done enough.

Orbán saw himself as being under constant attack from the Soros empire since 1992, by various means, under the surface. Soros is behind at least ninety percent of the accusations of anti-Semitism leveled against him, his government and Fidesz. The accusations of opposition to democracy that were made during Orbán's first term in office—as well as since 2010—are also at least ninety percent attributable to the Soros empire.

Between 2010 and 2014 there were also very serious problems about how this whole network was exerting pressure through organizations that had not received a legitimate mandate from anyone, especially the electorate, but which could still influence the actions and room for maneuver of individual states and nations. For example, there were the so-called "independent" credit rating agencies. It is worth looking at how, during the first Orbán government, these agencies reacted to, say, a Soros article on the Russian economy and the stability of the ruble; or how they reacted when a minor bank panic broke out in Hungary in autumn 2011 as a result of a sentence or two dropped in the foreign press. Soros pressed a button, and the credit rating agencies sounded the alarm. As had been the case in autumn 2008, in 2011 there was an attempt at a life-threatening attack on OTP, but this time Soros used the credit rating agencies as his proxies.

. . . .

And the activity of Soros networks was proven a thousand times over after the adoption of the Media Act. There was no opportunity for a substantive debate. A machinery was set up that proved systematic and overwhelming. Such was the size of the creature created by Soros that only part of it needed to be controlled, while the rest — through indoctrination or simply automatically — did its work and brought energy to the conflict.

. . . .

The Soros empire is a professionally constructed, largely self-operating network, some of which really does not need to be directed, because conviction makes it what it is. Things happen because Soros's troops really believe that those are the right things to do. In their fight, no amount of evidence or facts mattered: what confronted Orbán's government was an unrelenting, ruthless, massive machine, immune to persuasion.

When we talk about the Soros empire, the Orbán–Soros battle, what is most important is not first and foremost Soros's vast organization, but its ability to amplify its messaging when required by the situation—or to turn down the volume when its interests demand. In other words, it is the press, the media, the talking heads, the intelligentsia: they are the forces with the power to protect interests and amplify messages, and ignore or silence opposing voices. Even in America in the early 2010s, one could hardly find any articles that lifted the lid on Soros. Anyone who "stooped" to writing like that was peripheral and "extremist," and was ostracized from the circle of serious people. In other words, such a person would be committing journalistic suicide. This is still the case in Brussels today. The mainstream opinion-forming elite, including the media, consigns such approaches to the category of fiction: "Soros? The tooth fairy!" Cue for laughter all round. The name Soros cannot be uttered, even in the midst of the migration crisis, because the response will be that anyone who calls out Soros is an idiot, a conspiracy theorist, or even worse: they are evil.

So there is an ongoing battle in—and for—the media. In Europe now we have reached the point at which there is no media for politics anywhere—except in Hungary. And here in Hungary, it started with the Left having everything. Under the Horn government (1994–98) there was only one newspaper that was not in the hands of the communists: *Magyar Nemzet*; and of course even that was subject to pressure from them, and it was a red-letter day if anything could appear in it that did not correspond to their narrative.

This was the point from which Orbán started. Then along came Brussels, which experienced a rude awakening. "Something is happening here which is moving in the opposite direction, and it must not be allowed!" The heat has been on ever since.

. . . .

Orbán's brilliant insight about Soros was to understand that the key to all this is in the judiciary. This is why, after 2010, Orbán has said: "Let there be a new constitution, let there be a new constitutional court, let there be judicial reform; because everywhere Soros has tried to get in through the judiciary, and has used that to wreck everything."

In America the Soros name has become an expletive not because he has used money to enter politics. It is not because he has virtually taken the Democratic Party into private ownership. It is not because he has invested a great deal of money in trying to bring down certain politicians (Bush and later Trump) and to put others in office (Obama and Clinton). All that is simply natural: that is how things work. The scandal arose when it became obvious that Soros had entered the judicial system and started interfering in the appointment of prosecutors. Uproar ensued when it became clear that Soros had penetrated the deep structure. This is the essence of Soros: opening up the judiciary and entering through it. This is how he gets into everything—including the European Union. One of his great successes has been the setting up of the European Public Prosecutor's Office, and the installation in Brussels of European Chief Prosecutor Laura Codruţa Kövesi. He chose Kövesi—who is Hungarian in name only—while she was under criminal investigation in Romania. Today we have a Sorosist as European Chief Prosecutor—who, of course, is constantly complaining that she does not have enough powers. So in taking over the judiciary, Soros's aim is to dictate what the norm is. It is also to infiltrate the local courts in those jurisdictions where his network is threatened, in order to protect his agents against the imposition of the norms he opposes.

Orbán was already aware of all this.

It was no coincidence that the document Orbán's government was drafting in 2010 was not called a constitution, but the Fundamental Law—the name of which echoed that of Germany's *Grundgesetz*. This is Soros's terrain, and it did not escape the attention of his system, which immediately set off alarms. Who allowed Orbán to create a constitution? It was true that all the EU countries had done the same earlier and that was considered fine; but who allowed Orbán to do it? The Hungarians were not even allowed to breathe independently! Viviane Reding, one of Soros's top people in the EU, harassed Orbán for five years. But by the time they realized how things were playing out, the Fundamental Law was a *fait accompli*.

After 2010, every move Orbán makes will create a precedent and is therefore intolerable: if what Orbán does ends up being an example for others to follow, then a state of mortal danger will exist. Hungary itself does not matter and no one cares about it. Orbán could have built a nice little closed society on these 93,000 square kilometers (36,000 square miles, around the size of Indiana or Portugal), and if he had not wanted to be both a precedent and a counter-example, there was a good chance that he would have been left alone. But if what Orbán is doing is also offering the world an alternative proposal—well, that cannot be allowed!

. . . .

Up until 2014, however, the whole liberal Western world thought that Orbán would lose the 2014 election anyway—after all, in 2010 he had taken over a bankrupt country. Soros was sure that Orbán and his people would be unable to manage things well and to avoid failure. He thought it would be enough to keep the opposition alive, fund them, and then they would come to power. When he saw Orbán's government, Soros imagined a kamikaze-style government like József Antall's: he thought they would bleed to death as they tried to repair the economy. But what Orbán already had in mind was a ninja government. The teeth that would be knocked out and that he wanted to see on the ground were not his own, but those of his opponents. Because, after all, it is better to destroy one's opponent than be left dead on the battlefield.

2 0 1 4

The Devil never sleeps, but occasionally he snoozes.

In 2014 Orbán won the parliamentary elections again with another two-thirds majority, and then won the European Parliament and local elections. Again the country would turn orange, Fidesz's party color, and the sky would fall! In 2014, Soros realized that this could be a real problem: if Orbán could win in 2014, he could win again in 2018, and then he would stay in power.

Four days after the local government elections, the troublemaking began. There was the US travel ban scandal.* Street protests were initiated, and the US Embassy took the lead. This was when they realized that they had slept through the past four years, and there was a problem. So an attempt to overthrow the government was launched, during which there was continuous coordinated action between the US Embassy and the Soros network's organizations in Hungary.

Although we do not have any factual data on whether the Old Gentleman was turning the screws himself, it is certain that the US Embassy in Hungary did not carry out any action without prior coordination with the Soros organizations operating in Hungary. So any US action, statement, or demonstration that was launched after the 2014 elections could not have taken place without the Soros network being informed.

The situation was life-threatening. An opportunity opened up for Soros to intervene and bring down Fidesz and Orbán. The cat saw that now, perhaps, it could venture onto the tin roof. That was when it first became apparent that perhaps the conflict should be brought out into the open. In Orbán's witch's kitchen, serious consideration was given to meeting force with force, cutting to the chase

---

* "Hungary's tax chief says she is on the U. S. travel ban list: paper": https://www.reuters.com/article/world/hungarys-tax-chief-says-she-is-on-us-travel-ban-list-paper-idUSKBN0IP10J/ (Accessed May 2, 2025).

and launching a national defense action plan—including a point on expelling Soros.

In the end this did not happen. There might have been the strength to do it, but the right moment did not present itself. Orbán felt that the time was not yet right.

....

But strength was growing. In 2002, defeat had come in the form of a lesson from above. It was such a failure that the only way to deal with it was to learn from it.

After the defeat Orbán asked his new adviser, Árpád Habony, if he would be Prime Minister again. Habony said: "Not as Viktor Orbán, but as a regular guy from Felcsút." Which, loosely translated, means that you should not forget who you are, where you came from, what you owe and to whom, and what you mean to the people.

Another thing that needed to be learned from losing the election was that there is no golden age, we never arrive, we are always on the road, and politics is one long journey with no end in sight. The worst thing that can happen to you is that you believe your own story, you feel that you have arrived, you have finished the job, you have no one to learn from, and you have won. Because victory is never final: you always have to fight for it, it is not given to you, and you have to go into battle for it. So conflict and struggle is not bad: it is good, because with it you may prevent a greater conflict, greater strife. So good governance alone does not win elections. You have to engage in politics. You have to build a conflict—which in turn will build you— and you have to lead from the front. You must always be on the offensive, because if you are on the defensive you stand a good chance of losing. Continuous attack is risky, but without risk there is no success. And if you do not succeed, people will not stand with you and you will have no chance of winning. So in the aftermath of failure in 2002, this—together with other similar Orbán rules—was distilled into a lesson from above.

Experience later came from many places. This was partly about one's own experience and partly about what one needed to learn from one's opponents. For example, how to organize oneself in the way that they do. Then, to have what they have: organizations, institutions, civil society organizations, a base, media, talking heads, your own CEU ("Mathias Corvinus Collegium is our Central European University").* Have these within the borders and beyond them. Make the necessary "peace treaties": one cannot afford to have war within one's own ranks. Then one has to organize the civil society sphere: initially this was the "civic circles," bringing in soldiers from where they are; and one has to be able to channel their anger. At the same time one must build one's own sphere of experts and intellectuals. Then have this think tank and that research institute: one needs to develop alternative metrics, a democracy index, new scales of evaluation and validation, and some adjudicating experts and institutions. One needs a confrontational media platform on one's side, like *Megafon*.** One needs to do what Soros's people do.

Through years of hard work, Orbán has done it: he has built a systematically operating machine that has been able to show its strength.

. . . .

After 2010, from his position in government, Orbán was also able to benefit from increasing strength. In the space of about two years, he moved beyond the problem of having to solve crises overnight, to beginning a process which aimed to build national autonomy and sovereignty. It was not certain that

---

* "Mathias Corvinus Collegium (MCC) is an educational institution and research center devoted to the flourishing of the Hungarian nation": https://mcc.hu/en/vision (accessed March 26, 2025).
** "An initiative to defend against attempts to intervene from abroad and a place where right-wingers can confidently voice their opinions": https://magyarnemzet.hu/english/2022/12/megafon-battling-the-dollar-liberals (accessed March 26, 2025).

it would have come together in a way that was obvious to everyone at the time; but the way the Hungarian economy was led out of the crisis put Orbán in a position in which the task was no longer to break the shackles inherited from the previous economic structure, but also to prevent those shackles from reappearing. So Orbán got some breathing space and room for maneuver. This allowed him to literally and figuratively "whiten" the economy (i.e. suppress the "black" and "gray" illegal or informal sectors). This not only meant many billions more forints going into the Treasury, but also the closing of a number of loopholes in the Hungarian economy, resulting in a narrowing of the playing field for those not on the inside — in other words, their ability to exert influence was reduced. So not only did these steps reduce Hungary's vulnerability, but they also limited the penetration capabilities of all foreign actors. Their loopholes were locked shut. A system was set up that started to move at the systemic level; and when something moves at the systemic level, anomalies are pushed further out to the margins.

In this narrowing playing field, Orbán followed the logic that if one digs a pit and a nation falls into it, then of course the most important thing is to get out of the pit; but once you are out, you must not stop, but instead start to climb the hill. This is all part of an active process. And in the meantime, never forget who led you into the pit, because otherwise you could have forged ahead with a pit's worth of the time and effort you just spent on getting out! And when they started to look around for those who had been responsible, the former government — i.e. Ferenc Gyurcsány*—was in the front row, immediately ahead of the Brussels elite and the world of the ringleading pro-Soros NGOs. So, in parallel with the expansion of sovereignty and room for maneuver, the Soros problem would come slowly into view.

This strengthening allowed Orbán to assume a posture of resistance when the Soros civil society organizations and

---

* Left-neoliberal prime minister, 2004–09.

NGOs started to rant. Orbán simply refused to budge from his position just so that they would change their opinion of him. From Orbán's point of view, this conflict was about these Soros-funded organizations whose main aim was to prevent the realization of what he wanted to happen. He did not want to have this type of interference, founded as it was on interests based outside the borders of the country.

Orbán's intentions in this regard have been vindicated by all the geopolitical initiatives and power-grabbing attempts of this period. Ten years after the 2004 Orange Revolution, riots erupted again in Ukraine: a color revolution reloaded. Orbán saw that Soros had in fact been surrounding Russia with a ring of fire. Descriptions of the various revolutions and riots that have followed the same playbook, named after various flowers, could fill a botanical encyclopedia. And whether something is a riot or a revolution—in other words, whether it should be viewed negatively or positively—is something that is determined for the world by Soros organizations and the journalists in their pay.

Orbán saw that Hungary was also being surrounded. Very serious administrations were falling, from one moment to the next. In 2013 half the Czech government was taken into police custody, and the Prime Minister was accused of complicity in a corruption scandal. Orbán's Slovenian comrade-in-arms Janez Janša was forced to serve a prison sentence as a result of corruption charges. The anti-corruption prosecutor's office was used to decapitate the political elite in Romania, where one government followed another so quickly (one lasted a mere seventy-eight days) that it was hardly worth remembering ministers' names. In Bulgaria, too, it is hard to recall how many times the leader was removed. All around us, prime ministers were being thrown out of office from one moment to the next, simply because they were judged not to be going in the direction they should have been going in—and in some strange way they were always replaced by people who were linked in one way or another to a Soros organization.

The pressure within Hungary was unpleasant for Orbán, but it was the examples from abroad that tipped the balance—or at least sounded the sirens. "If you are not alert, you will be overthrown. There will be no mercy shown to a government that thinks beyond the current election cycle and in terms of national sovereignty. If you cannot defend yourself, Soros will knock you off course."

. . . .

Orbán had his "weapons" that could be used to take on Soros successfully.

Such weapons were the support of more than fifty percent of society and a two-thirds majority in Parliament—i.e., political stability. The Fidesz–KDNP alliance governed alone. There was no need for a coalition, and with a two-thirds majority it could make decisions quickly. Moreover, people were taking to the streets—but on its side, and not against it. This was the political significance of the so-called "Peace Marches."*

Added to this was an incompetent opposition. Soros could not find a foothold. And Soros is not stupid. When such people—very smart, tough people who can comprehend very large systems—realize that those they are working with and supporting are incompetent losers, they can drop those idiots overnight. Much later, in the 2022 campaign, Soros's people in Hungary said that Soros did not want to give money to the opposition's prime-ministerial candidate Péter Márki-Zay. Soros did not think he was up to the job: roughly translated, his opinion of him was, "I've thrown back smarter fish."

From these two factors come a third: active resistance, which means not only that Orbán does not allow himself to be bought or suppressed, but that he himself is capable of taking the initiative—and has the strength to do so.

---

* The tenth of these took place in 2024, with hundreds of thousands of participants.

Therefore Orbán's resistance is much more effective than the defense Soros comes up against elsewhere. It is true that from the start the Chinese excluded Soros from the game, the Russians—and later the Croats—declared him *persona non grata*, the Belarusians also expelled him, the Uzbeks closed the local Soros office for a while, and the French found him guilty after fourteen years of litigation. But it was Orbán—with the backing of a two-thirds political majority and the ability to turn an incompetent opposition into a competitive advantage—who would throw down the gauntlet to him in a way that would become a worldwide issue, an international furor and another huge story. As a result, the whole world would be talking about the duel between Orbán and Soros.

. . . .

In 2014, or a year or so later, Fidesz were holding their traditional birthday party. At one point during the celebrations, Orbán and his friend Zsolt Bayer struck up a private conversation. They talked about taking a look at themselves, all the way from 1988 into the not-too-distant future. They were shocked to realize that they were among the few survivors from the generation of activists that overthrew communism. "But the fact that we exist," said Orbán, "is most probably because we've never sold out; we're a community of friends and brothers-in-arms in the truest sense. And, not least of all, we're not afraid to show one another our backs, knowing that we can go to war together and won't be stabbed from behind."

Uncle George, that very clever man, was definitely wrong about one thing. He believed—and his whole life is testament to this belief—that money could buy everything, and that it was just a question of who would cost how much. He did not realize that here, in the middle of Europe, there are some people who are not for sale. Soros still does not understand how this could be.

UNSPECIFIED YEAR
....

It was Plutarch who said that there could be value in view-
ing people's lives in parallel. Through the similarities and
differences we can understand something of the world, of
the nature of things; we "simply" need to be judicious in
juxtaposing the lives of great people. We need to know who
is worth comparing with whom, and whether the people
we choose really are comparable. If we keep this in mind,
our analysis will not be arbitrary.

Plutarch believed that the heroes of Greek and Roman
history, with their vices and virtues, taught us to recognize
the limits of human nature and political knowledge, and
that a trivial incident or remark often sheds more light
on someone's character than the greatest battles, armies,
or sieges.

Plutarch viewed the great figures of Greek and Roman
history in parallel for a variety of possible reasons: because
of the similarity of their virtues and sins; to compare their
differences; because the second imitated the first, while the
first approved of the second; because they had a common
destiny; because they both owed their rise to power to
inherent greatness, or one came to power and succeeded
through the will of the citizens, while the other did so
against their will; because one was a favorite of the gods,
while it seems that the very birth of the other defied the
will of the gods; or because one represented one truth and
the other another truth.

....

There is an American saying that if a Hungarian follows
you into a revolving door, he will come out ahead of you.
But what if two Hungarians go through the revolving door,
and the revolving door is the world? Which one will come
out first?

Viktor (Orbán) and Soros. Viktor is a masculine name,
derived from the Latin *Victor*, or "winner." Soros is an

assumed name which, in Esperanto, means "will soar." Esperanto, incidentally, became a tool of the secret services, and Soros's father was one of its greatest Hungarian exponents. So there are two Hungarian people here: one a "winner," and another who "will soar." In age they are separated by the lifespan of Christ (thirty-three years), yet their involvement in politics starts at about the same time. Both started out at the bottom, although that is true of most people. Soros left Hungary with a suitcase at the tender age of seventeen to become one of the richest and most influential men in the world. Orbán came from a small Hungarian village and propelled Hungary onto the world's front pages. Both are very clever. They are so smart that each even recognizes the intelligence of the other. Soros thinks that Orbán is a very talented and clever man, and Orbán thinks that Soros is a clever Hungarian. Both are seen as "big beasts" in the old-fashioned mold: men who will make history, and about whom history will be written. Both Orbán and Soros are self-made men: they are where they are because of themselves, their talents, their abilities. One is a guru, the other, Orbán, is referred to as "the Boss." They do what they do with ease. But just because they make what they do look easy, this does not mean that what they do *is* easy. It may be very difficult, but they do it with ease, because they have the talent and the necessary experience.

One is an accidental stock trader, and the other is an accidental politician. Here "accidental" means "for lack of something better." Soros wanted to be a philosopher—a great philosopher. Orbán wanted to teach at a university, he wanted to do something with his law degree. And then, for lack of something better, "accidentally," one of them became a billionaire stock market shark, and the other a record-breaking prime minister, the most important Hungarian politician in the last hundred and seventy-odd years—depending on where you start counting from. Perhaps the reason they are so successful in their careers is that neither of them has been welcomed in by the intelligentsia. Neither of them is inclined to forgiveness. Both sleep very little and work very hard. Both Soros and Orbán make their people work, but they do not ask more from them than they give themselves. They give their all.

They are said to be surrounded by an aura of both history and charisma. Both are loved and hated. Whoever loves one hates the other. This is another sign that they are adversaries. Hating a stock trader is something that the soul can somehow come to terms with, but it is far more difficult to love a politician. Orbán is perhaps the only modern European politician who is genuinely loved and adored by the people, while Soros is regarded by the people as the Devil himself, his every move accompanied by contempt and derision. For the elite, the reverse is true: Soros is the good guy, the philanthropist; Orbán is the Evil One with cloven hooves. The perception is that one is fighting on the side of the people against the elite, while the other represents the contempt the elite have for the people. And if there can be two alternative truths at the same time, then each can be both an angel and a devil.

What can be confidently assumed is that each stands alone as a result of his power: two men of great stature, two giant redwoods. The trunk of each has been scorched by forest fires. Both Soros and Orbán want to succeed and avoid failure. Both think that the world has been waiting for them and that it is their duty to improve it—and that truth cannot be defeated unless one's diabolical opponent cheats. And the Devil always cheats. Therefore one must be better prepared, smarter, stronger, and better organized than one's adversary, and there is always an adversary. Both Orbán and Soros need enemies.

Politics is a game, and the winner is the one who can surprise the opponent. Even the most formidable opponent has a weakness, and everyone is afraid of something. Therefore fear is the safest terrain on which to attack the other. Neither of them likes to be on the defensive: they like to attack. They also know that the hardest thing is retreat. Both believe that there is no success without risk, but the chances are greater than the doubts, and all that is needed is to be clever, bold, unconventional, wily, cunning, and tough. These two men use methods that others do not. They are the ones who take the risks and make it possible for others to follow in their wake. They forge a path across untrodden ground and say, "Follow in my footsteps!" It is that simple, that is the recipe. They also say that one must seize the moment, because it will not return, and that experience is more important than anything else. They look not only at what is happening, but at what should happen. Of course they know what will happen eventually; but they also want to know what will happen in the meantime. They are people who frequently look down at our world from a satellite, from where they can see where the clouds are swirling. When playing Monopoly, they are not the short-sighted ones: if they roll a "double one," or land on "Go to Jail," they do not give up, but say, "Well, soon enough I'll just roll a 'double six.'" They both possess a necessary dose of ruthlessness.

This is why, in China, Soros is called a crocodile (it is an ancient observation that crocodiles shed tears when they eat, and for many centuries it was believed that they mourn for their prey); and in Hungary the post-Kádár intelligentsia call Orbán a tiger, a ruthless predator that stalks its prey, toys with it, and dispatches it mercilessly. According to one of them, if one cannot change, if one cannot renew oneself, one must die. Another says that if eight puppies are born, seven must be thrown into a river. Both can endure more than any of us. They can take the pressure. This is why they have an instinctive distrust of everything and everyone. Perhaps this is also why they will only believe their own eyes, but are not at all reluctant about learning from everyone—always, from anyone, whenever and whatever they can. One thing they instinctively know is that the world is too complicated and needs to be simplified—and they are well aware of their ability to do so. There are those who are benevolent and those who are malevolent. Those who do not stand on this side stand on the other side. They are very clever and very aware of what is in their interest. And so there is conflict between them.

But while Orbán, like a boxer, likes to fight face to face, Soros — similar to the Czech knight in the epic Hungarian poem *Toldi* — likes to fight from behind and by tripping his opponents. Orbán fights in public, in front of the electorate, while Soros fights behind the scenes, hidden from the public. Orbán competes and puts his faith in the ballot box, while Soros has no intention of trusting the people with his fate, and bets on his money. Every move Orbán makes falls within the constitutional order: he believes that the rules of the game can only be changed by legal action within the constitutional order, and only if one is authorized to do so. Soros says he has just enough money not to be subject to the law, and for the rules of the game to be embodied in him. Orbán says that a strong person can always name at least five or six things that they would never do under any circumstances. Soros, on the other hand, would certainly never say that there could be something serving his goals that he would not do.

Orbán always seeks stability, so that he can stand on his own two feet and not be overthrown. But Soros prefers situations in which there is imbalance, instability, or chaos, because you can fish well in troubled waters. According to Orbán, you must fight for what is right with the majority behind you. Soros says that he is right, regardless of what the majority wants. Orbán says that the most important thing is sovereignty: to be able to decide matters for ourselves. But Soros says that this creates the unacceptable risk that things could go wrong: we could end up with regimes that are sovereign, but closed. Thus, he says, there is always a good reason to intervene. Orbán thinks that a pile driven into firm ground is more solid the more blows it receives. And Soros thinks that a pile driven into the sand only needs a little help to be pulled out.

If we had a time machine, and Orbán were a Roman lawgiver, he would build a temple to Fides (the goddess of fidelity) and Terminus (the god of boundaries). But Soros would build one to himself. According to Orbán, the border must be protected, because without it there is no organized state. According to Soros, borders must lose their meaning and the world must be opened up and be as one. Orbán opposes immigration; Soros supports it. Orbán stands on the base of Christian civilization; Soros believes that no culture has a privileged place or importance. Orbán believes that family is family; Soros says that anything can be a family. Orbán is someone who believes that a good person puts their country first. Soros thinks that such a person can only be bad and dangerous. For him freedom has no homeland, because it is at home in the whole world.

So there are two opposing forces in the world, and they are now embodied in two Hungarians. All the major conflicts in the world today are distilled in the confrontation between these two. There are two flags, and one can stand behind one or the other of these two flags. Orbán holds one of them, Soros the other.

Now, the situation is complicated by the fact that one thinks that the other owes everything to him. He was where things started, he helped the other get started, he smoothed the other's path, he was the other's second father. For this he should be thanked, not stabbed in the back.

Plutarch wrote that there had not been a single parricide in Rome for almost six hundred years. The first parricide after the Punic Wars against Hannibal was committed by Lucius Hostius. His name is preserved in memory.

It was time for the duel.

The Duel

2015

This is the most important year in this story. It was a turning point in the struggle between Orbán and Soros, but also a turning point in the fate of Europe. A new crisis reared its head, and modern-day mass migration began. Millions were setting out for Europe, with one illegal immigrant arriving every twelve seconds. This marked the start of a series of terrorist attacks in Europe's major cities. Terror found a home in Paris, London, and Munich. A new struggle was beginning, one in which what was at stake was the survival or disappearance of our way of life, our values, and our European nations.

Éva now lived and worked in South Africa. János Betlen was retired, but still helped out here and there as a translator. Gábor Horn appeared on television as a fierce critic of Orbán. Gábor Fodor had become president of the Hungarian Liberal Party, which he had founded, and a member of Parliament. The SZDSZ and the MDF were no more. Formally the MSZP still existed, but no one understood why, or how this was possible.

This was the last year in which Soros visited Hungary, and he decided that he would never set foot in the country again—because Orbán is the Prime Minister.

....

"Events change everything." This American saying is about how things can be changed in an instant. It seemed that Orbán and his government had a knife at their throats, and that now it had really been decided that they would be taken down. The pressure was enormous. And then, suddenly, something happened. In Paris, on January 7, two Islamists carried out a mass shooting at the editorial offices of the French satirical weekly *Charlie Hebdo*. Twelve people were killed and eleven others were wounded. Europe was in a state of shock. World leaders expressed their condolences to those bereaved by these barbaric acts. Orbán also expressed his condolences. But this was not all that happened.

Orbán tried to understand what was happening and why. He believed that mass migration and illegal immigration to Europe went hand in hand with terrorism, and that there was a direct link between the two. Because a skillful politician deals with issues where they are most tangible, Orbán used this assertion to construct a policy. He launched a national consultation on immigration and terrorism. Billboards were erected all over the country, each emblazoned with one of three outrageous slogans: "If You Come to Hungary, You Must Respect Our Laws!"; "If You Come to Hungary, You Cannot Take the Jobs of Hungarians!"; "If You Come to Hungary, You Must Respect our Culture!" This would generate a huge outcry. Orbán was saying that terrorist acts are proof that Europe is handling immigration badly.

This created a new battlefield that changed everything in an instant. A migration debate was opened up, raising questions such as whether to preserve or abandon our shared Christian culture. Shall we decide whom we want to live with, or shall we let a decision be taken externally by others, who will impose on us groups of people who are alien to us? Will nation-states remain, or will they be dissolved by immigration into some kind of supranational entity—into, say, a United States of Europe, an empire that does away with ethnic homogeneity? Must we put behind us the family, the nation, and Christian culture, because they are obsolete? And, because they represent a strong identity, do they always cause trouble? Or is the reverse true? Can only a strong sense of identity protect us from being invaded by an alien culture? Because a land that is being invaded cannot be welcoming.

These and similar questions were raised, and a battlefront was opened. On one side were the forces that wanted to stop immigration, with Christian culture, the nation, and the family on their flag. They do not want parallel societies, and they do not want immigration. On the other side were the pro-immigration forces, who were loath to respect the decision of those who did not want to accept migrants (despite the fact that this was a democratic decision), and who therefore wanted to put down the rebellion by all possible means: mandatory quotas, threats, blackmail, and procedures claiming the antidemocratic nature of their opponents. On one side Orbán; on the other side Soros. But the latter could not be named, and was not visible.

....

So a front has opened up, with no compromise possible between the opposing camps. Those who say that immigration is irreversible cannot yield to it, because the nature of irreversible things is that once you have made a mistake, that is the end: it cannot be undone. Germany could be reunified, but once you become an immigrant country, that is the end: the *status quo ante* cannot be restored.

The debate is about our future. The question is whether the country our children will live in will be the same country as the one we lived in. Will the same spirit, civilization, culture, and way of thinking define the character of each country, as it did in the time of our parents and grandparents, or will it be something completely different? This is what is at stake in the migration debate.

The pro-immigration camp says that action against migration is simply wrong. They say that it is not just impractical, but also immoral, lacking in any moral justification. Therefore the border fence must be torn down, and migrants must be allowed in and given the opportunity to mingle with the different peoples of Europe to create a "new quality." The anti-immigration party responds by saying that we do not want parallel societies, we do not want population replacement, and we do not want to replace Christian civilization with a civilization based on different foundations.

Reconciliation between the two camps is impossible. These are two different concepts, two diametrically opposed worldviews, between which no bridge can be built. For one camp, immigration is a question of coexistence; for the other, it is a question of border defense. For one camp immigration is the future, which cannot be avoided; for the other, it is a bad approach, which one must opt out of.

In fact this problem arose because the pro-immigration camp said that no one could opt out of this: everyone must become an immigrant country, whether they want to or not. So the heart of the migration debate is really a question of national sovereignty. Do you have the right to decide for yourself how and with whom you want to live?

. . . .

The fact is that we are the heirs of the Middle Ages. The essence of the Middle Ages is simply the struggle of Good against the forces of Satan. This is where everything is decided. It is within this framework that we tell our stories.

American politics in particular can be considered the most faithful heir to the Middle Ages. "We," says America, "are the Good who mean well, and we're opposed by the malevolent forces of Evil. How do we know that they're Evil? Because whoever opposes Good can only be Evil! And against Evil, all means are justified and permissible." This is how America became the world's self-appointed dispenser of justice, which it remains to this day.

This is pure medieval thinking. But this self-image is unsustainable. We cannot admit that we are the heirs of the Middle Ages, so we have rewritten the past: for example, we claim that the Middle Ages were a time of "darkness." It is difficult to call the Renaissance dark, while the Age of the Enlightenment was a time when enlightened people murdered one another—but we should not get bogged down in such petty details. The rewrite was a success. So we are not heirs of the Middle Ages, but of the Enlightenment: we are enlightened, open-minded, liberal, democratic, freedom-loving, beneficent, and charitable people who feel responsible for the world and seek what is good for everyone.

But this is the very definition of Soros! He is the philanthropist, the good man who wants to make the world a better place. Soros is Good. And anyone who attacks the Good can only be Evil.

This is a mechanical puzzle that cannot be solved by force. We need another solution.

. . . .

There are two kinds of mechanical puzzles: those which must be assembled, and those which must be disassembled. Soros saw the nation-states as a mechanical puzzle that had to be disassembled: they had to be dismantled, smashed, pried open. There was a mechanical puzzle confronting Orbán: how to assemble a sovereign state in the middle of Europe, which is capable of defending itself in the face of constant attempts to influence it. How can one do something that is different from what others are doing?

. . . .

Democracy: yes. Liberalism: no. In a nutshell, this is Orbán's "theory of the state." It is a sacrilegious statement, because it says that a democracy is not necessarily liberal. And anyone who commits sacrilege will be stigmatized and excommunicated. The intention behind thinking outside liberalism is that if everyone is seeking a way forward, then something different must be experimented with. Liberal democracies are finished: we need to look at what kind of state can succeed in a new world order in which everything is fluid and in motion.

In the post-1989 order, therefore, liberalism — as a school of thought based on dogmas such as that democracy can only be liberal — is obsolete. It states that Russia can only be an enemy of the West, that the Right in Central Europe can only be fascist, that international interests are more important than national interests, that international organizations are more important than nations—and that Soros is a philanthropist who wants what is good for the world.

Orbán proposed the antithesis of this: illiberal democracy. Everyone was outraged. An illiberal democracy is one in which liberals do not win, and Soros loses. According to Orbán, the liberals are finished because they have turned their backs on the national principle, on shared culture, and on the traditional concept of the family. Liberal open-door policies have left Europe defenseless against immigrants, let in terrorists, and then concealed the truth from the public, from the people. Indeed, it is forbidden for the truth to be spoken. The liberal elite thus opposed the people, and liberalism opposed democracy. And Orbán sided with the people and with democracy. The truth is that he did not have to change position to stand on the side of the people, because he has always stood on the side of the people. For three decades, unchangingly.

This is the same battlefront as that which has emerged on the migration issue, but fought in the language of ideologies. You could say that an illiberal stands with the people, defending the homeland, preserving national culture, rejecting outside interference and empire-building. And an illiberal picks up the gauntlet thrown down by Soros, and shows people the true nature of the philanthropist.

1 8 3 0

Stendhal's advice is that if you go into a town where you are unknown, you should challenge the most popular man to a duel. This is one feature of Stendhal's 1830 masterpiece *The Red and the Black*. As in roulette, you may or may not find success, but at worst the spectacle of the combat will obscure its futility. Because the only things that matter are strength and individuality. These are the only things that mean something to us as readers or observers of history. Just as Stendhal's work is a *Bildungsroman* recounting the personal development of its hero, albeit with a tragic ending, so this entire Soros affair has set Orbán on a path to world fame.

Orbán challenged Soros to a duel, the popular man took up the gauntlet, and from then on there was no turning back: Orbán was on his way to world fame.

....

The issue of the duel involved the problem of how to present it. Could Soros be named? Could he be openly challenged? How much could one even get involved in a global ideological conflict? These were the questions.

Orbán spoke to many people at the time, and everyone opposed a public challenge. Rudolf Tőkés, a Hungarian historian and political scientist living in America, told Orbán that he could not enter into such a thing with any chance of winning, because it would always be little Hungary that no one knew and that was not important to anyone. Therefore Hungary could be outmaneuvered at any time, and if any talented prime minister of this small country challenged the world-beating Soros — who is backed by huge wealth, resources, influence, and power — to a duel, then they simply could not win.

Orbán's American adviser, the Republican Arthur J. Finkelstein, was also against the challenge. On one occasion, when a political scientist in a meeting with Finkelstein said that he was leaving early because he had to go on television, Finkelstein pressed him on the topic. The answer was "Soros." Finkelstein was beside himself, exclaiming: "That's off limits! That's absolutely forbidden! You don't know how powerful that man is, and how much damage he can do!"

Many other smart people in addition to Finkelstein have said that it is in our own interest for Orbán to continue fighting as he fought in the past, and to avoid engaging in open conflict, because that is a losing battle. They have said that in this political water polo match the kicking, fighting, and pushing should continue under the surface of the water, but Orbán should not commit himself to doing the same things above water. But Orbán thought that such a strategy was not good, because continuing like that would end in defeat, and that could lead to huge trouble.

It is part of Orbán's character that he has always liked to approach a given issue differently from the way in which others have approached it. He always looks at things from the other side of the table, or chooses a different perspective, from which things appear in a different light. The general view is that we have looked at something from a certain angle, and that is how things will continue. Orbán, on the other hand, goes to the other side of the table and looks at it from there, too, to see if it looks right from that viewpoint. Only after he has done this will he start to think in strategic terms. If you say something to him which conforms to the mainstream, he will say, "Well, everyone says that." If everyone pushes the same message, it will not work, but if one person looks at it from the other side of the table, that can work. This is what happened with the question of Soros: everyone was against the idea of having an open conflict with Soros, while he thought it was the right thing to do.

So it was Orbán's idea to name Soros, and that was typical of him: no one else would have dared to attack Soros, because no one thought that far ahead. Of course this was a serious strategic decision, but Orbán is capable of making them—and that is another difference between him and everyone else.

Orbán set about putting his intention into practice. First he convinced László Kövér, then the Fidesz party board, and then things took their own course. Orbán was convinced that this match could be won if it was played above water. He believed that if he made the conflict public, if he introduced the real Soros to the public, then Hungarians—the majority of them—would be with him. As Soros's assets in the underwater battle were multiplying and Orbán's were not, Orbán was increasingly convinced that such a battle could not be won. But Orbán did not want to lose. He said that he had to fight above water and invite people to join in this conflict. His argument was the following: "No one will defend us except democracy, because we only have as much power as we get from the people. So it's best to present the whole conflict to the people—this is the fair approach. In terms of democratic principles, it means showing people that there's a conflict here: 'We're up against an organized force, and the result of this will directly affect you. You have the right to know about it.'"

Obviously, timing is important in this. Just think of the patience and determination needed in order to wait two decades to exact revenge. Orbán felt that he had made the right decision at the right moment—just when a decision of this type could be taken. It was no accident that he did not do it immediately after 2010—although he felt the urge to do so even then. So he waited for the right moment, and he waited for the right occasion: the migration issue. He entered the right conflict at the right moment, with the right power behind him, and he knew what he was doing. He was also sure that publicity was a force that would help him.

....

There is a Fidesz rule which says that when you get into a complicated situation, you have to explain to the world what the story is: "We do this, the other side does that, and the outcome is this and this." It is not even necessary for Orbán to have the last word when determining this narrative, but by describing the situation he makes the conflict understandable to people.

Another Fidesz rule is that to do this you do not necessarily have to manipulate the facts, because it is enough to describe reality fairly. In other words, reality—the facts—helps the side which is disclosing it. It is an objective external force that gives additional credibility to the narrator. This force is then embedded in a collective unconscious, creating the feeling that "We are so right that we simply cannot lose."

. . . .

The entire Western liberal worldview—its mode of thinking and language framework—has been shaped in large part by Soros, and its influence and appeal signifies his intellectual and other influence. This has been so strong that it has been very difficult to counter it, or even to argue against it. A good indication of this is that when, in 2014, Orbán came up with his plan for an illiberal state, the headwinds he faced were hurricane-force. The moment and the occasion for a showdown had not yet arrived, and it was only in 2019—five years after the idea was announced—that Orbán would be able confidently to justify his own proposal. Soros has never engaged in open conflict, always having helped behind the lines in the name of certain values. He fought in politics in such a way that he was always underwater: you could not see him, and you certainly could not say that Soros, the Soros network, or the Soros empire were behind anything. Such words were impossible to say in international politics, and would immediately elicit loud accusations of conspiracy theory, anti-Semitism, and the like.

It was to Orbán's credit that at one point he said—and this was during the escalation of the migration conflict—that his side would not accept that way of fighting. A halt would have to be called to the water polo match that had been going on up to that point, in which everyone was playing by the rules above the water while under the surface there was no end of dangerous rule-breaking. So enough of that! The people had a right to know who George Soros was and what he wanted. So then Orbán suddenly showed who is behind the pro-immigration flag. He said: "Let's drag Uncle George out into the sunlight!" And that turned out to be a good tactic; because if there is one thing Soros hates, it is sunlight, and that kind of publicity.

There is a key document on the migration conflict that Orbán occasionally takes with him to Brussels in his pocket, so that if he is attacked there, he can pull it out like a jackpot lottery ticket. The background to this started when, after the migrant invasion of Budapest in the summer of 2015, Orbán wrote an article outlining his six points for dealing with the migrant crisis. Barely three days later, Soros responded: the website *Project Syndicate* published Soros's own six points, which were then immediately published in Hungarian. In his article, Soros wrote that what Orbán had written was not good, and instead his own recommendations should be implemented: Europe needed Soros's six points. With this, however, Soros made the conflict personal. The formula was resolved into "Orbán or Soros. You have to choose, because only one of them can be right. On this issue there can be no peace, there can be no agreement; there is nothing to agree on, because even to compromise is to admit defeat." From that point on, the issue of migration was made clear to the whole world by its personalization. Soros wanted to encourage it; Orbán wanted to stop it. The cloak of migration was thus placed on the shoulders of the duelists, the whole arena was defined, and the story was made comprehensible to everyone.

....

Sometime in 2015, Zsolt Bayer and his colleagues were sitting in the editorial office of *Magyar Nemzet*. Suddenly the editor-in-chief, Gábor Liszkai, came in and said: "Confront Soros—no more pussyfooting!" Zsolt and co. were so angry at Soros's incessant provocation and troublemaking that they could not wait to lay into him. Yes, they knew that it was really a mechanical puzzle, because while Soros is indeed the main villain, if someone attacks him then immediately that person is regarded as a Jew-baiting stinking anti-Semite. Zsolt's counter-argument was that Meyer Lansky was a mafia boss on a par with Al Capone, and a member of the "Jewish mob." "But," Zsolt argued, "if I describe Meyer Lansky as a mafia criminal, am I an anti-Semite? What nonsense!" Although Zsolt was right, when attacking Soros he could no longer be right. Every statement attacking Soros was put in the dossier marked "anti-Semitism."

1 9 4 1

Orbán's desk is always full of books. They are piled up on top of one another — open, stacked, annotated, dog-eared or simply laid aside. There is one slim volume in particular that has caught his interest, and reading it has been a joy for him. In 1941 C. S. Lewis wrote *The Screwtape Letters*, one of the most entertaining little books in Christian literature. In it the author discusses the Christian faith from the Devil's point of view, in the form of a collection of letters. In these letters, Screwtape, an older and more experienced demon, gives advice to his nephew Wormwood on how to tempt the soul of a believer away from the enemy, Jesus Christ.

Because not only is Great Disruption in progress, but also Great Deception. The Devil's soldiers are not commanded to do evil, but told that what they do is good. And eventually they lure the whole world into the delusion that whoever serves the Devil is serving the Good. One of the letters describes how the man who has been selected is almost converted. Wormwood is advised to make the man's stomach rumble with hunger. So he does, and when the man's stomach is rumbling and he is on the verge of conversion, he realizes he is hungry and goes out to get something to eat. And when he returns from the spiritual space to the human space, he realizes how close he was to thinking some ridiculous nonsense.

Uncle Screwtape's letter contains similarly convoluted logic, plots, and techniques — including the maxim that what matters is not argument but jargon. The Devil's mission is to befuddle you, to achieve permanent aggravation in your life. His servants do their best work when keeping certain things from our souls. Consistent and cool-headed routines are needed. Malice, Screwtape advises, must be directed to immediate neighbors who are met every day, and benevolence must be thrust out to the "remote circumference," to people we do not know. Human emotions, Wormwood is told, must be directed towards the future, which is why the Devil favors "schemes of thought such as Creative Evolution, Scientific Humanism . . . which fix men's affections on the Future, on the very core of temporality." Screwtape writes that "Nothing is very powerful," and that hatred is concocted by his side.

In other words, you have to twist and turn and deceive people until they believe that what is bad is good. Because, to use another phrase, "the justice of Hell is purely realistic, and concerned only with results," having no time for excuses.

．．．．．．．．．．．．．．．

The whole philosophy of the Soros world was to develop this by wrapping it in something else. And that something else was a particularly brazen challenge to fate: to say outright, "We are the saviors of the world."

Soros has a philosophy of life, worldwide success, a personal story, a vocation stemming from it, and—because he understands the function of this—he is clever enough to use it for his own purposes. So he turns his sails to catch the winds that are good for him: specifically, he brings American national interests—or even world-hegemonic interests—into synergy with his own interests, and packages them so that he can say they are his own. This is because his vanity means that he does not want the Soros label to fall off the packaging, and also because he does not want the American establishment to feel that he is working against them. The methodology and basic definition of this spectacle—or, if you like, Soros's rule number one—is that in no substantive way must what is happening be revealed. Sometimes, of course, the Old Gentleman's true nature can be seen through the fabric—as when he attacked the pound, when he tried to take down OTP, or when he bought into Macedonian mines. But he has tried to keep such things hidden. And there is also the argument that the Good is so good that it more than makes up for all that. This is the essence of the invented tale of philanthropy, which is told to us as if we were children.

Orbán dragged Soros out into the sunlight, showed him to the public, and said that Soros was a real problem—indeed the Number One! For Soros, this was the greatest sin that Orbán could commit against him.

This is because Soros really is Number One in the world—someone who can twist and turn, convert his money into political power without having to govern any country, compete, or take political responsibility. He has devised a much more sophisticated solution: he is every-where at the multiplier points, and he just gives the orders and pulls the strings. Clearly he has more power than a prime minister! He can take down a Macedonia in no time if he needs to. He can press the strategic acupressure points anywhere, and efficiently make the most profit with the lowest possible investment. The message or instruction he issues goes through his whole network—including the entire world media, down to Cambodian news outlets. And he does all this with about ten people. Meanwhile Soros is invisible: he cannot be spoken about, so he does not exist.

He is also present in Brussels—without being present. He hides his presence as if he did not exist. Of course there are meetings with the top leaders, where he is received with the signs of respect normally given to a head of state—which is only necessary because of his vanity. But beyond this Soros cannot be seen.

. . . .

So in Brussels, too, Soros is behind a veil. This is also true of his six points. They were blended into various EU doc-uments, including the Commission's proposals, and from then on they were never referred to as the Soros Plan. The dirty laundry has been washed, and the loose threads have been sewn up, to disguise the origin of the concept. This was the first step in the disappearing act.

Then came some more chicanery. The various NGOs began to publish points from the concept in the form of messages to one another. These were not examples of straightforward "copy-paste," as there was always a little tweaking, spinning, and modification, but the elements of content were the same. Meanwhile, in the course of these iterations the origin of the plan—where it came from—was again forgotten.

This was followed by a robust campaign in the European Parliament, with ever more political groups putting the issue on the agenda. But again, arguments and points of view were moved around—as was how to deal with the subject. The Alliance of Liberals and Democrats for Europe (ALDE) saw Soros's points as a human rights issue, and the Social Democrats as a question of labor shortages and social inclusion. But, as once again the plan was dismantled and each party backed it up with its own set of arguments and narrative principles, the great planner himself had long since disappeared from view. The situation was more complicated in the European People's Party, where "Roger, Wilco!" was not the accepted response, because within it there were different schools. The Mediterranean countries, for example, were happy to support a mandatory migrant quota, but as one moved closer to Central Europe, the situation changed. So the method followed there was to amplify the voices of the supporters—a strategy which was guided by the Germans. This is how the Soros Plan became the European Parliament's position, while completely losing its Soros complexion. And so when Orbán came out with the claim that Soros had a plan, again there was laughter: "Whose plan and what plan?"

Soros also realized that it was all very well to exert pressure on Hungary through America, but in Hungary's case it would not be enough; EU pressure would be more effective, because that is where the money was, that is where the financial sluice gates were. Those gates could be closed, and so it would be more effective to harass Orbán and Hungary through the EU. Soros's realization was that the Georgian government should be pressured through America, and Hungary through Brussels. Therefore the stock of the Soros alumni in Brussels has risen.

Moreover, Soros focuses on the EU without having to give a penny. He is seen in Brussels as a big donor, but in reality Soros uses Brussels to finance his projects. This is also a synergy: Soros needs the project so that he can have an army and have it financed, and its soldiers look up to "their George" with stars in their eyes. Of course when it leaks out that a host of MEPs are Soros's people or are even on Soros's payroll, it does not become a worldwide scandal: simply nothing happens, there are no consequences, things just continue as before. "Whose people? Come on!"

But what are these people like, these people who are "obviously not Soros soldiers"? Soros soldiers are certainly dupes. They are people who believe in something unquestioningly, but are extremely naive. Some are childishly naive and some are aggressively naive. The latter are the particularly hateful ones. They often drag academics along to support them, whose job is to add credibility to the message. But it is the childishly naive ones who do the day-to-day work; they are the ones who are willing to give their all for implementation of the Soros Plan—and this is why they were chosen. The job of Soros's people has been to amplify Soros—even as they conceal Soros himself—and to build up intellectual capital so that decisions arrive "pre-cooked."

Their job has been to demonize Orbán.

From the very beginning, however, this demonization lost its factual character. The image of Orbán they have drawn is built on people's natural fascination with mysticism. There is the angel who is Soros, protecting vulnerable people, giving them money, working tirelessly to spread all that is good. So there is a selfless elderly man who, despite his advanced years, is putting a lot of energy into making the world a better place. In comparison, Orbán is the evil Eastern European. What kind of people are Eastern Europeans anyway? Indigent latecomers, barbarians whose continual interference in the West's affairs has prevented the West from changing the world for the better—something it could have done long ago. Orbán is quite simply an evil man lining

his own pockets and seeking to stop this decent, philanthropic, generous old man from pushing through his agenda
for global improvement. Orbán is stealing the money that
the Westerners give him and—leading the Hungarians on,
taking advantage of their gullibility—is building something
monstrous. And all this is because he is evil. The story of
Orbán's objections to migration policy has never been fully
told. No one cared what arguments he had, or what factual
claims were made by the Hungarian side. Instead there is
Good and there is Evil. Orbán is the cloven-hoofed Devil,
who—in this forsaken country in the back of beyond—is
using all means possible to overcome the Good, to defeat
Soros. Obviously this must not be allowed to happen.

....

It is true that Orbán has also employed guile, knowing full
well that only cunning works against cunning.

Soros has always been concerned with the question of
immortality. In an interview he once said that his real goal
is to outlive himself. Soros has always wanted to be a philosopher, and to be remembered for his ideas.

In Western culture the home of ideas is the university.
Soros founded one himself, based in Budapest. CEU—or
the Soros University, as Orbán and co. call it—is at the
heart of the whole Soros phenomenon. As one of his people
in Budapest said, CEU is Soros's most important political
legacy, his main project, that which lends him legitimacy,
the jewel in his crown. And this is what Orbán attacked.

Soros would react with uncharacteristic recklessness to
what he saw as a provocation. It was Orbán's decision that
the Soros University should not be attacked on ideological
grounds, although that could have been done, but in terms
of legality and the rule of law. The government pointed
out that all universities should be subject to the same laws,
but that during Gábor Fodor's time as education minister
Soros had gained privileges for himself—and together with
his associates he wanted to maintain this privileged status.

The government then said that all that was over, and the school should be integrated into the Hungarian legal system in the same way as all other Hungarian universities. The matter should be seen through, whether or not they liked it. So Soros suffered a blow, and he took up the gauntlet: he made an ideological issue out of the university issue. So there was a conflict of interests, which in an instant Soros turned into an international conflict. The perception that in Hungary there was a battle between the government and the Soros world—and even between the Prime Minister and Soros—spread across the world.

Orbán would later say that he thought that the Soros University was the best episode in the entire duel. In fact political disputes of this nature are called "microparticles": they are not particularly important in themselves, and it is one's opponent who decides what they turn into. Soros should not have reacted to this, but it was a matter that was close to his heart. He loved being here in Budapest, he had an apartment on the top floor of the CEU building, and he liked to take long walks in the city center, sit on the terrace of a restaurant and eat a good *pörkölt* (Hungarian meat stew). No one would recognize him, and he had no bodyguards. He felt at home, he felt young. He felt that this was his city, his country. How could Orbán do this to him? After this, Soros could no longer come to Budapest; he could not, and did not want to. He was very hurt by what Orbán did to him and by the consequences. His operations had been immobilized; he had been challenged; he had begun to be hated. This was what he could not bear.

For Soros, his Hungarian project was a personal matter. He had set himself the goal of disproving the saying that one cannot be a prophet in one's own country: he wanted to be a prophet in his own country, and he wanted to be the greatest prophet there. It was therefore a great personal insult to him that his university's headquarters had to relocate to Vienna. But, as Orbán said, "We're not discouraged or saddened by this."

So Orbán hit Soros where it hurt him the most, in his heart. Soros wanted to leave a Budapest-based CEU to the world, but then Orbán came along and brought the curtain down on the dream. On top of that, Orbán even put up a billboard of the Devil, showed his face and said: "Here he is, the Evil One."

Soros could not tolerate this. What was Orbán thinking? How dare he? Soros made the university issue a world issue, and then Orbán saw that it had been written everywhere — including on his own forehead — that the Hungarian government was anti-Soros. Soros had made him a world star, and he would be almost unknown in the wide world if George Soros had not built a brand for him with the Soros University — a brand that since then has not weakened.

2018

You cannot squeeze toothpaste back into the tube.

The duel was over. Orbán had won. He had won this year's Hungarian election — again with a two-thirds majority. Now the whole world could see that Fidesz had been Uncle George's worst investment.

On June 20, 2018, the Hungarian parliament voted on the seventh amendment to the Fundamental Law, making an addition on combating illegal immigration. On the same day, the parliament adopted the "Stop Soros" package. In August Soros moved the offices of the Open Society Foundations from Budapest to Berlin, and in December he was named "Person of the Year" by *The Financial Times*. And Orbán annoyed Soros by talking about planning as far ahead as 2030. By that time, he says, Hungary would be standing on its own two feet, with a sovereign government, and the Soros empire squeezed out. By then Soros would be a hundred years old, and if he lived that long he would have to see Orbán still in office as Prime Minister of Hungary. This is called giving the Devil a heart condition.

The following June, CEU held its last graduation ceremony in Budapest. George Soros's son Alex, a member of the CEU Board of Governors, conveyed greetings from his father to the graduating students. CEU was moving its headquarters from Budapest to Vienna, saying that it had been chased away. (Despite that claim, if you walk around downtown Budapest, to this day you can walk past a beautiful and imposing building with "CEU" in huge letters on its facade proudly proclaiming its continued existence.) Soros received the Ridenhour Courage Prize. It was not presented to him by Orbán.

In 2018 Soros was 88. There was news — they do not want it to be widely covered, but something has to be said — that he was transferring eighteen billion dollars of his personal wealth to his foundations. In other words, Soros was settling matters with the US government. The ratio was 20:80

(twenty percent privately-held assets, eighty percent publicly-held assets), allowing them to remain in the foundation system. This was proper and correct, as is normal in the West. Sometime in the 1980s, Soros received a huge sum of money for "soft power" political subversion. He did this work and made a lot of money from it—and so he not only spent money, but also earned it. And towards the end of his life he was told, "Well, this much is yours, you can take it home, it's your private property; but you have to leave the rest in the system, and your son will manage it." George out, Alex in.

Plutarch wrote somewhere that the more a son gets from his father, the less he can achieve himself. Orbán felt that this was a wise thought.

. . . .

According to the medieval Church, sin is the result of the Devil's wiles; and therefore man must be constantly on guard against the Devil's temptation. The perpetual lure of temptation is that those who bargain or associate with the Devil gain enormous wealth and supernatural power. But in our folk tales, the Devil can be defeated. Those who are able to do so typically achieve it not through greater physical strength, but through greater intellectual strength. Those who win do so because they are cleverer than the devils or outwit them—as, for example, in the Hungarian folk tales "Hetet egy csapásra" ("Seven at One Blow") or "Koplaló Mátyás" ("Starving Matthias"). In the latter, the devils pronounce their final judgement: "Rather than ruining ourselves, let him have the hundredweight of gold; for Matthias is a greater devil than any of us."

. . . .

What does victory mean?

Orbán outsmarted Soros. Through guile, wit, shrewd ideas, and maneuvering, he has broken the image of Soros as a well-meaning philanthropist who supports everything good in the world. Until now this had been an insoluble mechanical puzzle which everyone failed to crack. Because if you attack a good person you can only be bad, and if you attack good principles you can only do it in the name of evil. Moreover, Soros is a Jewish person, and anyone who goes after a Jewish person is also an anti-Semite: "Game Over. You've lost—Soros has won."

Orbán outsmarted Soros by opening up the game and making it all public: introducing Soros to the public, and making it clear to everyone what the nature of the battle was, and what was at stake. Up to that point everything anti-Soros had been ideologically discredited; but the spell was broken by publicity. An increasing number of people began to feel that what Orbán was saying and doing was explanatory and based in fact, so that anyone who attacked Soros was no longer a member of a sectarian minority.

Moreover, Orbán not only introduced the real Soros to the public, but also invited the people into the conflict. He launched a national consultation and held a referendum on the migrant quota, and the message of the subsequent election was that the voters should decide whether the government in Hungary should be formed by Soros or Orbán. The people backed Orbán. The national consultation on Soros produced a record turnout, and the migrant quota referendum—although falling short of the required turnout to be legally valid—opened up a huge political market: more than three million people backed Orbán, and the next election resulted in another two-thirds majority. It turned out that the biggest force is that of attraction, and what attracts people is strength.

But bringing this conflict out into the open required not only Orbán, but also Soros. Soros has gained money and influence everywhere he has intervened, and everywhere he has succeeded he has acted rationally. In such circumstances he is a seasoned professional, ice-cold, and with zero morals. Orbán, however, had goaded him with CEU, he had pierced the old gentleman's heart, and Soros flipped. He responded to the challenge and took a public swipe at Orbán.

Paradoxically, Orbán was helped by the fact that he was not in the same weight division as Soros. It really was a David and Goliath fight. Here was the prime minister of a country of ten million people; and no matter how talented he may be, his country was only ten million strong, with the economic power, GDP, and vulnerability of a country of ten million people. And he was up against a modern-day Goliath: a powerful man who had orchestrated who knows how many crises in who knows how many countries, with similar scripts, similar actors, similar interpretations—and financing centers. However, by being attacked by Soros, and becoming his "Enemy No. 1," Orbán's power was now not only his own, but also that of everyone else who was Soros's opponent. And, of course, the reverse was also true.

Orbán won by reversing the logic of the fight against Soros. When, for example, the Russians blacklisted Soros, the message was that he was equivalent to America, the CIA, the intelligence services, and all that. But Orbán gave this a new twist: he did not say that it was the US secret services that were making trouble, but that it was Soros. Orbán gave the whole struggle a personal face, and in doing so he translated it for everyone, making it comprehensible. Today, nowhere do they talk about the CIA or the deep state doing this, but they talk about Soros. This is also what they say in America.

By featuring Soros's face on billboards, Orbán has also said that he is the Evil One. So Soros is not the Good, and this is not about philanthropy: this is about Soros wanting to destroy us, wanting to incite migrants to come here, wanting to disrupt the social order, wanting to dictate how we should live. We must stop Brussels, and so we must stop Soros. With this duel, Orbán has become a global player, an international star, a global poster boy; because whoever defeats a global poster boy becomes a global poster boy himself. Orbán has joined the big boys:

in 2019 all of them met him, because they thought they needed to.

But behind this is unparalleled courage. Taking on the hegemon? It is not openly said, but he took it on. He could have been shredded. Orbán could have been sent to prison, as happened to a number of other prominent politicians around us in the Carpathian Basin.* And this was the plan: before the 2022 elections, there was talk in public that if the Hungarian opposition won, no planes would be taking off, everyone would go to court, there would be confiscation of property, a simple majority would change laws requiring a two-thirds majority, and Orbán's constitutional order would be abolished.

What would have happened if Soros had won? We can see that—more or less—from today's Poland. But what is certain is that, as a first step—and in the spirit of internationalism, virtue, the search for common solutions, cooperation, and solidarity—he would have implemented the rules and mechanisms that Orbán had vetoed in Brussels, and in one fell swoop Hungary would have become an immigrant country. At the same time we would have gained a good reputation in the international media, we would have been back at the forefront of democracy, and we would have even received pats on the head and praise from Brussels. Then Soros would have gotten his money back. After all, Orbán's economic policy—what might be more appropriately called "sovereignty policy"—has caused the old gentleman serious financial loss. He would surely have reversed that, because why would he want to make a loss? And we Hungarian voters would have paid the price. In the end, he would have made sure that it would never happen again: "Hungary needs to know its place, shut up, and put a yes-man in charge."

---

* The geographical region in which Hungary is located, and which before 1920 belonged to the Kingdom of Hungary, also known as the Pannonian Basin.

....

Why has this struggle become paradigmatic?

Despite the success of resistance to Soros in other places, such as some of the former Soviet republics, those examples have not become paradigmatic. It is also interesting that no influential precedents were set in Malaysia, the former Yugoslavia, or Turkmenistan. Hungary has become such a precedent. This is not because of Trump, but because of migration, with Trump only coming later.

Orbán was the world leader in the fight against Soros. No one before him in Western democracies had ever committed to open conflict with Soros. Soros had his conflicts in the East and in the West. He even drove the British pound down, yet then the British chose to fight under the surface of the water. In the West, in the transatlantic world, Orbán was undoubtedly the "icebreaker," who said: "Come on, get into this match!" But if you get into a match, you cannot afford to fight halfheartedly, because then you are finished. Here is another Orbán rule.

And here is still a further rule: if we do not know what we are fighting against, then we cannot influence the fight in our own favor. So it was necessary to look at what the Soros phenomenon was, and what its greatest strength was. The answer lay in its systematic nature. There is the idea, derived from Karl Popper, that anyone who puts their nation before other nations—either in his heart or in his mind—is in essence bad. It is difficult to call this a very illuminating or complex idea. So it is not a question of intellectual power, but of Soros being able to select people who can cope with a Sisyphean workload, who can be integrated into his system, who can be taught Soros's way of working, and who are capable of systematic work. This demanded a huge amount of money, and Soros got a huge amount of money for this purpose. So he had no problem with the budget. But after all it was his own talent that enabled him systematically to build an empire that did its work systematically. The Soros empire gets up, does its work, goes to bed, then wakes up again the next day to start all over again. Every day it gets up, works, goes to bed, gets up, works, goes to bed. The army of Sorosist troops put in x hours of work every day. So Soros's greatest strength is systematic work and numbers: a lot of people in a lot of places, well organized, coordinated, with an internal communication system, and working every day. It is very difficult to mount a defense against this, because it is a big machine—it is like a road roller slowly but surely coming towards you, on course to crush you.

The secret of Orbán's victory is that he recognized it for the road roller it is. It is a road roller that moves forward inexorably and cannot be stopped by a single action. A road roller cannot be forced off course with a motorbike, but only with another road roller. If you want to defeat it, you too must build an inexorable machine: your road roller against Soros's road roller. You have to put in as much work as Soros puts in. You need as many people working for you as are working for him. They have to work for as many hours as his people work. Orbán's principle is that his people have to get up every morning, work, go to bed, get up the next day, and do their work. This is the only way, because in order to get to the shore, you do not need to pray, but to row.

The way the Roman legions operated was that every last move and piece of equipment was planned out—from setting up camp, to marching, to fighting in battle, to retreat. Absolutely everything was organized and well thought out to the last detail. When Rome was at its peak, a Roman legion could only be defeated by another Roman legion. This was the essence of the battle between Pompey and Caesar. A systematically and carefully constructed system can only be defeated by an equally systematically, carefully constructed and ruthless system.

But the poor countries of the East cannot organize their own governments in this way—let alone defend themselves against Soros. For this reason alone, individual actions could not set a precedent. According to Orbán, Soros's attacks on Hungary failed because here the state-building instincts and capabilities are strong. Soros may have thought that this was Eastern Europe, but in terms of state-building capacity, constitutional thinking, and culture of governance, this is a Western country with a tradition of governance that has taken root over the course of more than one thousand years.

But what Orbán has done is to show the whole world—from Buenos Aires to the Hungarian village of Nemesmedves—that it is possible to fight Soros, and that it is possible to fight him successfully. You simply have to be sufficiently persistent, brave, smart, educated, and determined. Because up until Orbán, everyone rolled themselves into a ball and accepted the fact that the Soros organization was engaged in meddling and chicanery. No one had dared to take up the gauntlet until Orbán openly accepted the challenge.

So what is happening in the fight against Soros is the same as with illiberal democracy: it has become a precedent. The message is, "Believe me, my friend, if I could do it—and we're just a country of ten million people, like a drop in the ocean—you can do it too, because you're much bigger and stronger." This is why it is important to go to the Argentinian president, the Brazilian president, to all of them. Even to meet with the prospective US president (Donald Trump), who credits Orbán with being Europe's strongest leader on an almost weekly basis. It is no coincidence that *The New York Times* is already writing that the alliance between Trump and Orbán is extremely important for 2025, for the world as a whole. Both are anti-immigration, both reject liberal democracy, and both want peace in Ukraine. By contrast, we can safely say that Soros supports immigration and liberal democracy, and wants to continue the war. So, once again, it is Orbán or Soros.

The bottom line is that American soft power politics no longer defines Hungarian politics, and that since Orbán defeated Soros the roles have been reversed. This is perhaps the most astonishing development ever. Returning home after visiting presidential hopeful Donald Trump in early 2024, Orbán said the following to Hungarian TV station M1: "In America today Hungary is seen as a special place, a place that's different from the rest. They see Europe today as one big liberal, progressive, liberal ocean. And there's an island in it, a single island: this is Hungary, which is trying to live differently, think differently, and behave differently. Let's say that it's pursuing conservative politics in the same language as them. And it's not just talking about it like America, but acting on it."

Orbán has become an extremely popular "cult figure" in American conservative circles. The Republican Party is even said to align its platform with him, and Trump considers him a strong ally. When I asked the German-American screenwriter Collin McMahon—who has worked for Disney, among other studios, and is also the author of important books on Soros—how he sees Orbán from America, he described Orbán as the cornerstone of European conservatism and of resistance to the Soros agenda. It is very important for Fidesz to work with MAGA Republicans in the US and with other patriotic governments around the world to expose the Soros network and NGOs like Action for Democracy that use illegal election interference to attack democracy in Hungary, among other countries.

So Orbán is a cornerstone, a point of reference, a key figure, an international star who shows the world the direction in which to go. Is it good to be on the world map? Comrade Kádár thought that it was good for Hungary to be on the front page of the world's newspapers only in connection with Olympic gold medals. Perhaps there is something in that, but it is not yet clear who is right. In any case, Orbán has become famous around the world for defeating Soros. Because, although Hungary does not matter and no one cares about it, what Orbán is doing could be very dangerous—because, for example, Argentina, the whole of Latin America, and India already matter a great deal: what happens there matters a great deal.

In India, too, Soros is stirring things up: he is supporting anti-India movements and elements, and doing everything he can to weaken India's national and nationalist character. To do this he is using the NGOs he funds, the media, and the intelligentsia. But we already know this story, as Soros does the same thing everywhere and is trying to interfere in India in order to achieve his aims. Soros—who sees nationalism as the main threat to the world—sees Prime Minister Modi's efforts to create a Hindu state in India as a dangerous step backwards. Soros is doing everything he can to ensure that Modi does not succeed. But now India has taken up the gauntlet. In an interview, Minister of External Affairs Jaishankar has set about Soros in the same tone as Orbán does, with similar turns of phrase and insights: "Mr. Soros, an old, rich, opinionated person sitting in New York, who still thinks that his views should determine how the entire world works. Now, if I could just stop at 'old, rich and opinionated,' I would put it away. But he's old, rich, opinionated, and dangerous.... He actually thinks that it doesn't matter that this is a country of 1.4 billion people . . . whose voters decide how the country should run.... I cite him as an extreme example, but there are other manifestations of this in different countries, where people like him think an election is good if the person we want to see wins: 'If the election throws up a different outcome, then we actually will say it's a flawed democracy.' The beauty is, all this is done under the pretense of advocacy of open society, of transparency, etc." So an Orbán-inspired revolution, or a campaign of national resistance to Soros, is also taking place in India, the world's most populous country. The Hungarian prime minister's name appears in *The Hindustan Times* on a daily basis, and now—following the Hungarian example—Soros is being called out for what he is.

There is also a "Viktor revolution" in Latin America. When Orbán was in Argentina, not only the Argentine president but also the presidents of Bolivia and Paraguay asked him: "What now?" Everyone is looking at Orbán. At a meeting of the Organization of Turkic States the room was buzzing with the audience's chatter, but the noise died down as soon as Orbán started speaking.

Orbán is a superstar wherever he goes in the world. He is surrounded by an almost irrational level of devotion. They do not even know where his country is, but they take selfies with him in Buenos Aires. These are things that cannot be explained, and do not need to be explained. This is how it is, thank you very much!

....

How was Orbán able to win?

Speaking of things that cannot be explained, there should also be some explanation of how Orbán was able to defeat Soros. He won because he was brave. Who knows from where he drew strength, from what source; but he had the courage to take on the hegemon, taking on huge risks — including personal risks. He had the strength and the stamina to see the fight through. So personal courage is always the most important. He won because Orbán is a free man and Soros is a bound man. Orbán's commitment to freedom, to the freedom of his nation, has proved stronger than the bound interests of the bound Soros. He won because he was right — or it turned out he was right. On immigration and a number of other issues, Orbán was, is, and will be right, and Soros's position is untenable: a man who has no homeland cannot force those who do to abandon theirs. Or he won — as we have seen before — because he showed that this is how Soros works. In doing so, he has demystified him, and in world politics Soros no longer enjoys the immunity provided by being a philanthropic businessman who does good.

These are the more or less rational explanations. Those who see him, his people, also tend to come up with explanations of an irrational nature: that Orbán simply cannot help it; it is his cross to bear; he has been chosen for this task; and it is his destiny to fight what is bad and evil. Because God always finds some instrument, because He has to find an instrument to counter the power of evil, and one of these instruments could be Orbán.

So this explanation goes beyond human reason—if only because it is humanly impossible to endure this pressure. His close associates say that one simply cannot have such a nervous system. It is impossible: "He has nerves as thick as my arm." So there is no rational explanation for how he can bear it.

Today's people of great stature have one clear advantage and one clear disadvantage compared to people of great stature in past times: if all goes well, they have more time to accomplish great deeds, because the achievements of the modern age give them a longer lifespan than, say, Alexander the Great. The disadvantage is that they must exercise constant self-control, because the technological situation is such that they no longer have a single free and independent moment. This is unbearable pressure. Being a "big beast" today comes with unimaginable pressure. But Orbán can bear it, and does bear it—while getting hardly any sleep. From early morning to late at night he is talking to people, meeting with them, listening to them, and has some kind of thought about everything. And people love him. It is as if they have sensed something of the irrationality in this— because they love him irrationally. There is really not much rational explanation for this in today's desacralized politics.

． ． ． ． ． ． ． ． ． ． ． ． ． ．

What does Soros think about this?

One of Soros's people said that the Albanian prime minister—who is a very smart man, on good terms with both Orbán and Soros, and whose ex-wife is the head of the Soros Foundation in Albania—once asked Soros what the conflict between the two of them boiled down to. Soros tried to give him a casual answer: "Two smart Hungarians getting carried away—that's the essence of it."

Soros has always respected Orbán, admiring him for his brains. Partly, of course, it is because he feels he himself has something to do with Orbán's achievements and the fact that he has gotten to where he is. According to Soros's thinking, he financed Orbán's studies; if there were no Soros, there would be no Orbán, and there would be no Fidesz. And, of course, what Orbán did to him is in a sense parricide. He never dreamed that Orbán would attack his personal legitimacy, put his face on billboards, and force out his university. He felt that he was being mocked and humiliated for no reason.

Wesley Clark, the former NATO Supreme Allied Commander Europe and member of the Advisory Council of Action for Democracy, is one of Soros's most important people. In a leaked video* he has spoken about their powerlessness against Orbán: "Viktor Orbán is a smart fellow. He's been there thirty years in politics, he knows what he's doing. These people are hard to unseat."

And he is successful. For this reason alone, the Soros plans have not worked in Hungary, while elsewhere they have. The most important factor for Orbán is success. After all, the road roller of the Soros empire cannot be influenced by the truth: it can only be influenced by strength. What is needed is success. Orbán has said repeatedly—in America too—that the Right must understand that in order to win, historical and everyday truth is not enough: strength can only be proved through a mandate from the people—and the people want success, they want to prosper. The life of a country can only be well organized if the people know that if you lose, they too will lose: by your failure they will also lose something personally. If they feel that they have nothing to lose personally, then, in a mass democracy, people will desert you, and your success is over. Of course, Soros is also interested in success. But he can only win, he can only make color revolutions, if there is open discontent in society, if there is bad governance. So, apart

---

* https://videa.hu/videok/magyar-nemzet/hirek-politika/wesley-clark-tabornok-arrol-beszel-hirek-politika-eBFyaSndv8jm1beJ (accessed May 2, 2025).

from Orbán's inner conviction, the strongest motivation for good governance is George Soros himself.

There is a reason why Hungarian elections have been subject to interference and why there have been several attempts to remove Orbán, because Soros may also think that what Orbán is doing is a dangerous counter-example, into which a lot of organizational energy has been put. Soros knows that he is not dealing with a bunch of amateurs, and not even just a "ninja government," but with a well-organized army in which everyone knows what their task is. And the machine that Orbán has built is doing its job systematically, and it is extremely stable—if only because of the existence of enemies like Soros. In fact, the existence of Soros is one of the most important factors in its stability. And from this comes energy. According to Orbán, the little Hungarian only stands a chance against the great Soros if he multiplies his strengths and becomes a great Hungarian. This is a great Hungarian era. And Soros sees this.

As Soros's operations are now based in Berlin, where his people look at politics not only nationally but also regionally, he sees that what Orbán is doing is radiating outward. Its effect is primarily regional, but since the Dutch election we can now see that it has a European dimension, which could have consequences for power relations within Europe—and even across Europe as a whole. Because what Orbán is doing is spilling over to Poland, Slovakia, the Czech Republic, Slovenia, and Austria. This is understandable, but Orbán is becoming a reference point beyond Central Europe: in Italy and the Atlantic region, including in the Netherlands. Those who use Orbán as a reference point are capable of winning, and this is seen as a very dangerous thing, and something that is very wrong. Orbán expects the next stage to be a victory for Marine Le Pen in France; and this expectation alone shows that Orbán is more than a thorn in the side of the hegemon, more than a stick in its spokes.

....

Orbán is a dangerous opponent, who is standing in the way.

2 0 2 2

....

How do we know that Soros has been defeated? From Orbán's fourth two-thirds election victory.

....

A war is rarely over when it is officially declared to be over.

....

Plans are always upset by life. In 2020, COVID came into our lives and eclipsed everything else. The pandemic demanded that government bodies look at everything in terms of the virus, organize the state accordingly, and, through organizing the state, ultimately defeat the pandemic. Hungary was able to defend itself successfully against the virus because it had a policy of action: it had a government capable of action, and it had the political will to organize its defense. The politics of action had the strength and the knowledge to take the state organization into that war. It was able to get people to accept civilizational, social, and economic restrictions that affected everyone. The Hungarian state and the structures providing defense did not collapse (unlike, for example, in northern Italy, Belgium, or Romania), and they were able to cope with the pressure. The state, fighting the pandemic and forced into action, did not pass the test of perfection, of course; but it remained standing, and, when it came to lives, performed relatively well — if one can put it that way. And in the race to be the first country to present the image of a safe country, Hungary — thanks in part to its successful vaccination program — became a European leader, able to organize major international events in crowded but safe circumstances (the Euro soccer championship, the celebrations on Hungary's State Foundation Day on August 20, the visit of Pope Francis). The country was able to start up again sooner, removing restrictions and getting life back to normal.

Orbán also emerged from that crisis stronger. He seemed to be at full strength, with high hopes and big plans for the

2022 election campaign. Everyone was somewhat relieved, and we felt that we had gotten through the hard times, through two tough and testing years.

And then war broke out in a neighboring country— Ukraine.

....

No one cares about Hungary, and the fact is that no one cares about Ukraine either. The Russo–Ukrainian war was provoked—not necessarily by Biden's son acquiring land (and God knows what else) there, but by deliberately and knowingly failing to abide by the Minsk agreement, by deliberately violating it, and thus forcing the Russians' hand. They were backed into a corner, and left with no other option than what we see today. Because if they had done nothing, Ukraine would have become a NATO member, and then NATO would have been in their backyard. And if things had gone on like that, they would have had to give back Crimea—which would have been an unthinkable scenario for the Russians.

The fact is that Ukraine is a Soros project. It is true that no one cares about Ukraine. Ukraine does not matter; but Russia matters. Many years after his activities began, Soros said that the creation of the Open Society Foundations in the Soviet Union was his most important political act. He has invested a lot of energy and a lot of money in Russia, but he has failed. When Yeltsin was in power, Soros was unstoppable. Putin is unforgivable and intolerable because he was the reason that Soros had to get out of Russia. Therefore Ukraine was the springboard from which he could get back to Moscow. It had to be Ukraine because he had to get a foothold somewhere, having been forced out of several states in the post-Soviet space, and moving his headquarters out of Budapest—thanks in no small part to Orbán's efforts. His weight was therefore shifted from Hungary to Ukraine. The best thing would have been to move his university not to the Austrian capital, but straight to the Ukrainian capital.

Soros also realized that the key to the region, alongside America, was the EU. He saw that Brussels was impotent, and so he needed to be there to tell them what to do. And so Ukraine became a model project: a plan to derail Russia. It is difficult to find any other explanation for a sane person in Ukraine announcing that they want to join NATO, and it is also clear that the person announcing it did not do so on his own initiative. That person was himself invented. Let us not rule out accidents, but there is some reason to be suspicious: they made a TV series in which they showcased the "servant of the people," then they ran this servant of the people in the election, achieved power, and then made the announcement. Mission accomplished!

Orbán's position in this conflict was not predetermined. Some words of explanation on Orbán's intransigence are in order. Some years earlier, during the Arab Spring, when again Soros and America were the main agitators, József Szájer suggested to Orbán that he should go to Tunisia or Egypt, as other leaders had done: "Appear with someone there, make a gesture, say something nice." But Orbán refused, and it all came to nothing. At the outbreak of the war in Ukraine there was a similar atmosphere across the world, with the "evil" in your neighborhood that had been conjured up in front of your eyes with such great effort finally being induced to do its evil. In such a situation it was not at all obvious that the response should be "strategic calm." For this it took Orbán. For Orbán to dare to do this, it took the electoral situation in Hungary.

In both the Arab Spring and the Ukrainian–Russian conflict, Orbán was smart enough to ask: "Where are we running to? Let's see what the ten-year outcome of such a thing will be." This is a perfectly logical way of thinking, which is typical of Orbán: the greater the turmoil, the calmer you need to be. Then Orbán declared that sanctions were not working, that we needed a ceasefire and peace — and at home he won the election by another two-thirds majority against his Soros-backed and Soros-trained opposition. But his position left him isolated in Europe.

Soros approached the war as he approached all other issues: "There are the Good who want Good, and those who oppose this are Evil." Soros and an America led by the Democrats have succeeded in making the whole of Europe pro-sanctions and pro-Ukraine. No other position has been allowed, the possibility of reasoned debate has been eliminated, and anyone who tries to engage in it is pigeonholed as being on the side of Evil. And just as they had made a Herculean effort to build Russia up as Evil, the same thing has been happening to Hungary—in the present perfect continuous. Let us hope that the outcome will not be the same. Moreover, Soros—with this "good and evil" narrative, and by using the cliché that one has to be "on the right side of history"—has also succeeded in discrediting the concept of peace in Europe. The whole of Europe wanted to go to war, and Orbán—who, on the contrary, said, "Make peace"—was consigned to the dark side. This is, by the way, one of Soros's absolutely amazing skills. Russia has become evil, and everything in Europe has been wrapped in the Ukrainian flag. One has not even been able to watch a soccer match without seeing this stand taken. Orbán went against this, and was again branded as the Devil's own. "Those who support Ukraine are good people, just as you have to be philanthropic. But those who do not support Ukraine can only be bad people." This is "Soros logic."

Every week in Brussels the news that Moscow had done something was almost portrayed as if Orbán had done it. This message was fed right through the Western media, and a twin portrait took shape: Putin was the principal villain, and Orbán was his servant. Then a game started in Brussels, which can be described as "one against twenty-six": Orbán against the rest of the Member States. But Orbán believed that a game can always be turned around—even when it is twenty-six against one. Week after week, everything was about Orbán. He opposed sanctions, and he opposed the EU's plunging itself into debt by taking over a large part of the funding of Ukraine from America, and recklessly pouring that money into a bottomless pit. Orbán has also elevated the question of Ukraine's accession to the EU so high that the whole world holds its breath while it waits to see what he will do next: "Hungary can't keep defying the world! It can't keep defying the hegemon!" Imagine poor Joe sitting in the Oval Office, his secretary coming in and saying: "Mr. President, we have a problem, because Hungary is being difficult." "It's Orbán again . . ."; "Orbán said this . . ."; "Orbán isn't allowing the transfer of the money to Ukraine that you ordered." How is this possible? And this happens every week or two. It is a real and amazingly dangerous game of chicken. And in a game of chicken your opponent must look into your eyes and be convinced that you will not swerve off course. This is what Orbán's opponents see in his eyes, and it has a dramatic effect.

But Orbán knows what he is doing, because on the one hand the Ukraine conflict is about peace, how to get peace here again (well, if Trump wins, he will bring peace); and on the other hand it is a question of sovereignty at the deepest level—and again, it is against Soros. Because when seen in terms of formal logic, if there is a war there, and Hungary says what it is required to say (in line with the others), then at that moment you can expect a number of things: (1) troops will be stationed on your territory; (2) you must stop buying oil and gas from the Russians, which will make you vulnerable in energy. (As a result, the Russians would certainly not have dealt with us, we would not have gotten oil, gas, or anything from them, and we would have had to import shale gas and goodness knows whatever else we could, and at whatever price the Americans happened to be offering.) So if you say what you are required to say, from that moment on you are vulnerable in terms of both your territory and your economy. Whom will you be at the mercy of? The Americans. So what will happen next? What will happen is what the Americans want to happen. In other words, what you have been fighting for for thirty

years will collapse in a single moment. And although Soros
will not have managed to get in from here, there, and elsewhere, he will have managed to get in from Ukraine. This
is the risk involved.

Then they tried every means they could to push Hungary
into compliance. Every single day, Orbán was threatened,
blackmailed, and verbally attacked. Although Brussels
wanted to give money to Ukraine, it did not want to give
Hungary the money it was owed. There had always been
an objection to Hungary getting its money, but there had
never been any objection to Ukraine getting money. In
the end Hungary got its money, because the conflict was
too great. It turned out that the ones who were trapped
were not us, but Brussels. But the tug of war, the battle
of nerves, continues — as does the war, for the time being.
But to believe that Ukraine will win, one has to be either
in Western Europe or America; because in the rest of the
world that is no longer imaginable.

So history has not come to an end. The unipolar world
lacked an enemy, and therefore America lacked an ideology,
a cohesive force. In the final analysis, the Americans got into
this war for their short-term interests, whereas the Russians
seem to be able to think in terms of a long-term strategy.
Overstating the Russians' ambitions and underestimating
their true capabilities has proved to be a huge mistake.
And from Russia's point of view it seems quite clear that
the offensive in Ukraine is not about gaining territory, but
about breaking Ukraine — and, above all, the West. (At
first, of course, this war was about breaking Russia, but
the tables have been turned.)

It is certain that history itself has also been unfolding in
the present perfect continuous: it has continued into the
present and will continue into the future. This throws up
both opportunities and threats. Nowhere is it written that
one has to live in a liberal type of democracy — and especially not that everyone in the world has to live in one. The
depths that are opening up are dizzying and threatening.

Soros wants to restore American hegemony, and Orbán wants to say that you can be friends with everyone, you do not have to make exclusive commitments, and there is room for maneuver. This was also a message to everyone else, a message that everyone should do the same: "This is what you need to do, boys and girls; copy me and you'll be successful." This is the reason, for example, for such previously implacable adversaries as Serbia and Hungary suddenly engaging in unprecedented cooperation. How is this possible? This is just how it is.

. . . .

The battle with the Soros empire has not come to an end either. It is like a well-reinforced bridge, a system that cannot be taken down with a single strike. It is spreading its powerful toxin across Western Europe, in the Arab world, and in Southeast Asia. And the story continues. Those who fought in the Second Punic War did not know that just over fifty years later there would be a third such war. We, too, only know what the situation is now.

Orbán knows that Soros will want revenge, because he feels that Orbán has only won a battle, but not the war: "One of the reasons Soros is still alive is that he wants to defeat us at all costs. I understand this. He does not want to go into the hereafter without having taken out his opponent in the country that matters most to him. I know that I am dealing with an enraged man who is running short of time. Time is on my side, not his. He needs to win not only his battle against me, but also his battle against time. This means that in Hungary his efforts will increase in intensity. All people with such diseased egos feel that they are in a race against time, because they feel that they do not have much time and that what they have envisioned must be accomplished; and so they drive themselves to ever more radical and extreme behavior. This is the problem he has. And he is not constrained by any norms: Soros is capable of anything. In doing anything he can to achieve his goal, he is not constrained either by externally acquired norms—such as those we learn when we are brought up—or by inner convictions, such as belief in God or loyalty to a nation. There are no such constraints on him. At first sight one would think that this would make him stronger and better-positioned, but it does not."

Then there is Soros's son Alex, whom Orbán has never met. Alex has set about reorganizing the foundation system. He has been downsizing the Open Society Foundations' offices in Europe, one by one. Large-scale redundancies have taken place in London, Brussels, Barcelona, and Berlin. According to press reports, the cutbacks there will be around eighty percent, and around forty percent globally. The explanation for these radical moves is that Alex wants to concentrate primarily on non-EU territories, on the Balkans—and, of course, on Ukraine. And he is mobilizing all his resources to prevent Trump's return to the White House.

It has also been written that the Soros Foundation he wants to see will be far more political, more directly engaged in politics, than the one overseen by his father. And on his map, Hungary will appear in the same color as every other country. This has not been the case for his father: for "Papa" George, Hungary is his country, and he has a particular commitment to it. Alex has no such feelings: the boy just wants a simple victory. If he has any desire for revenge, or any kind of special anger at all in relation to Orbán, it is only because he clearly sees that this is where his father has most often been insulted—and boys take note of such things.

1 9 1 9

....

Everywhere across the world people felt that they were witnessing the end of an era. We had a sense of foreboding, we saw the disintegration of the former world, which we had thought was stable, and we unconsciously felt that we had been brought to the brink. As the visionary poet William Butler Yeats predicted, in his poem *The Second Coming*:

> Things fall apart; the centre cannot hold;
> Mere anarchy is loosed upon the world,
> The blood-dimmed tide is loosed, and everywhere
> The ceremony of innocence is drowned;
> The best lack all conviction, while the worst
> Are full of passionate intensity.
>
>   . . .
>
> And what rough beast, its hour come round at last,
> Slouches towards Bethlehem to be born?

Yeats wrote these lines in January 1919, two months after the end of the First World War. Somehow he instinctively felt that peace would soon give way to even greater horrors: what new kind of rough beast would slouch towards Bethlehem to be born?

....

Speaking of the First World War, the turning point of the war was not 1916, nor 1918, but the Russian Revolution of 1917 — because this revived Marxism. In the 1960s and 1970s, it was thought in the West that the Russian experiment was not a mistake, and that it could be done well — but that this meant going back to Marx. Karl Marx believed that the revolution needed to be launched not in the poorest countries, but in the richest countries. This is why the past few decades of the West have been under Marx's spell, and why Soros is in fact a new Marx. He, like his spiritual ancestor, has lost his soul, and his heart is animated and governed by a demon.

The co-author of *The Communist Manifesto* was studying in Berlin, having broken off his legal studies to switch to philosophy, while also writing poetry. Meanwhile his father experienced increasing desperation as he observed what was happening to his son's soul. In one of his letters he writes to him, "[Your] heart is obviously animated and governed by a demon not granted to all men; is that demon heavenly or Faustian?" His son answers this question in his poem "The Pale Maiden":

> Thus Heaven I've forfeited,
> I know it full well.
> My soul, once true to God,
> Is chosen for Hell.

We seem to be living through the last days of this ideological obsession, of this hellish world. But this world is no longer called Marxism; it is called the "liberal world order." But if you take the label off it, you see that—miracle of miracles—what is in the box is the same thing.

Those who still defend it are no longer of the stature of Jürgen Habermas or John Rawls, but tenth-rate figures. Their arguments are devoid of intellectual vigor, and what they say and how they say it has long since lost its intellectual force and self-confidence. Compared to the grand edifices of previous generations, their arguments are bike sheds, and merely the recapitulation of old texts. And although this liberal world is incredibly powerful, forging forward on its own path and unbelievably difficult to defeat, its intellectual content is now no more than a very thin, shoddy veneer.

Opposing this fractured intellectual order—and the Hungarian George Soros, perhaps one of its most important representatives—is another Hungarian: Viktor Orbán. The latter has built another intellectual and political world, which is increasing in power.

....

All the world's major conflicts can be described as a duel between the two of them. You only have to look at what is going on in the world today: Orbán opposes migration,

while Soros supports it; Orbán wants peace, while Soros
wants the war to continue; Orbán is for connectivity, while
Soros is for the formation of power blocs; Orbán defends
national sovereignty, while Soros attacks it; Orbán is a
democrat but not a liberal, while Soros is a liberal but not
a democrat; Orbán swears by the traditional concept of the
family, while Soros opposes it by propagating the notion
of "gender"; Orbán stands on the foundation of Christian
culture, while Soros stands on the foundation of nothing
at all. In both moral and political terms, all the issues of
our time come into focus when seen through the prism
of the conflict between these two men. Only very rarely
can such things find their embodiment. But now they can.

....

So Orbán systematically entered into a liberal–illiberal
struggle, consciously seeking to offer an alternative to the
existing dominant paradigm. He also knew that a paradigm
shift always provokes considerable resistance, and so he
would find himself confronted with an immensely more
powerful adversary. But in fact it was Soros who dragged
Orbán into this liberal-illiberal struggle, because Orbán
either had to fit neatly into the Sorosist ideological, intellectual, linguistic and political order or had to rebel. And
in such a situation, Orbán wanted to win.

So the struggle between the two of them can be understood as being between two opposing worlds, each with its
own foundations. But it can also be understood as a literal
battle, with each side looking at all the weak points of the
other and attacking wherever it sees a vulnerability.

All Orbán did was to think about how to organize power
on the basis of a majority in a democratic system. He
reasoned that his side wanted a majority, they wanted to
deprive the other side of their majority, and they wanted to
do it by attacking their weak points. Democracy is majority rule. Where his side was in the majority, they had to
besiege the other side on all the points that were already

serious problems for liberalism—such as LGBTQ and gender, migration, and issues related to societal coexistence. This strategy was necessary because liberalism was strong and was appealing for many people. So one had to look for points where attacking that liberal world revealed it to be less attractive, and enabled one to draw the majority away from it in order to build one's own majority.

Soros did exactly the same thing. He wanted to find the supposed weak points of Orbán's world: corruption, lack of solidarity in refugee policy, homophobia, Russophilia. He launched his attack on these points.

Orbán believed that this world could not be defeated by persuasion. So outnumbered was he that only politics could reverse the balance of power and strike Goliath in the face. In this he was helped by reality—which includes everything from biological reality (in humans the sexes are defined as male and female) to political reality (what can and cannot be done). Meanwhile Soros has brainwashing: to make his weak points attractive, he has had to work on people's brains. An example of this is the campaign against the death penalty in the US. When Soros and co. say that abolition of the death penalty is good because it makes you human, this is not something that people can directly experience themselves. Or there is the fight against Orbán, where they have done this work systematically. "I no longer need to tell you why you shouldn't cooperate with Orbán, because by his saying this and saying that, that ship has sailed. Orbán is evil itself, and anyone who says such things is evil."

At the same time, Soros has helped Orbán. In politics there is such a thing as bad publicity, but it is not always necessarily bad. Those who attacked Orbán actually helped to build him up: they were not only Soros's useful idiots, but failed useful idiots. Thanks to them, Orbán became world-famous. He became an international star with power, influence, and strong intellectual charisma. This was also Orbán's life insurance against Soros, because from then onwards, the Soros issue was no longer just a Hungarian affair.

....

Of course we Hungarians see everything through Hungarian eyes, and this is as it should be. But we think that this fight is about us, when in reality it is not. No one is interested in Hungary, and Hungary does not matter: we are a secondary battlefront. The main fronts are in Brussels and now in Washington.

Soros has received a great deal of money to carry out subversive activities in Europe, on the periphery, while keeping control of Brussels, so that American hegemony and its exclusive influence within the EU can be maintained. So Soros has occupied Brussels, he is trying to push the borders of this zone outwards, and he is organizing color revolutions here. In short, this is the task that Soros has been given.

What is at stake in the forthcoming European Parliament elections* is partly how much longer Soros can control Brussels — because Brussels is still in his control, although with every European election this control is weakening, and the grip is slowly loosening. So this is the most important thing at stake in the 2024 European elections. For the Soros Foundation also, the stakes are high. This is what the battle is about.

Meanwhile the EU is slowly weakening: it is losing its competitiveness, it has lost its capacity to act independently, and it is also proving to be inadequate at solving problems. The EU could be good and strong if it were about cooperation and taking advantage of the benefits of its single market. Strengths should be aligned and weaknesses remedied — this would be Orbán's policy for Europe. Instead, Soros wants a superstate that treats the individual states as provinces. The aim is to discard the world of nations, to classify the traditional concept of the family as Paleolithic,

---

* The 2024 European Parliament elections, held in every EU country between June 6 and 9, 2024. In these, Fidesz received a record 2.042 million votes, 45% of the total. (Official figures as of June 12, 2024, with 99.98% of the votes processed.)

and to abandon protected borders, letting in the destitute of the world to mix with native Europeans. In this weakened Europe, the US will have no difficulty in asserting its influence.

The years of post-communist transition are over, and the whole unipolar world order is at an end. Everything is being reordered, and in this reordering Soros's task is to put America in the best possible position. What this would mean for us is that Europe—including Hungary—would be brought down to and kept at a level that economically and politically subordinates it to American goals.

Hungary, however, is a borderland territory, the frontier of the Western world. If a schism occurs, we will be an insignificant periphery, just as we were in the days of the Soviet Union, when we were not important to either the East or the West. If this happens again, we will lose all our potential, and all the hard work of the last thirty or forty years will be wasted.

So what we are seeing now is the Hungarian response to change. There is a realignment, and Hungary must find its place in this realignment. Somehow the answer is not to become part of the American hegemony, but to take a position on the edge of the Western world that can draw all the resources from the East into Hungarian foreign policy and the economy—be those resources Russian, Arab, Chinese, or Korean. We need to draw in all the resources that are essential for us to have relations with both the West and the East. Loosely translated, connectivity means not being on the periphery. If the plan works, Hungary can cooperate with the West and the East in a way that no other country in the world can.

The plan is good. But why should others allow it? They will not. What is happening in Hungary is not only happening without permission, but is specifically prohibited. Major forces are being mobilized to ensure that Hungary cannot sustain this dangerous counterexample. The aim is to neutralize it as quickly as possible, and the situation is indeed life-threatening. Soros-funded media outlets are taking over structural positions in opposition politics, with the call going out to bypass opposition politicians. In early 2024 they launched an operation that would eventually lead to the resignation of the President of Hungary and the withdrawal from politics of the former Justice Minister and prospective lead candidate in Fidesz's party list for the European Parliament elections. The dogs have been set loose, and there is a real threat to life. Disobedience will not be tolerated. Every opportunity is taken to threaten, blackmail, or intimidate Hungary into compliance. Now it seems that we are not in a world like that of the Soviet–American world order, in which the two big powers came to an agreement in which one received permission from the other to "place its boot on our chest."* That is not the world we live in now. Now every country is important to other countries. Today we are important to America, but also to Russia, China, the Balkans, and Arab countries. Today is not like thirty years ago, when a great power could come and take you down. There is room for maneuver. And if Hungary is brave and clever enough, it can use this room for maneuver to its advantage. Orbán is working for this, and Soros is working to prevent this from happening.

Whether Budapest versus Brussels is a temporary phenomenon or will grow into a form of world order is yet to be seen, but alliances are being built. The America of the Democrats must pray very hard that Trump does not come back, because that could be a decisive turning point and have a decisive impact: if Trump returns, the war in Ukraine will be over and the European liberal mainstream will also be badly damaged.

Whether the path Orbán is following has a chance of success in the wider world depends to a large extent on others. It depends on the direction taken by the world; in

---

* The mutually agreed division of Europe between the great powers during the Cold War.

other words, on whether the economic and strategic trans-
formation of the world will strengthen the political forces
that, so to speak, have both feet on the ground. Put another
way, on whether the sovereigntists will be strengthened in
opposition to the globalists. If, on top of this, there is a shift
in power towards China, India, and the BRICS countries,
then the outcome is very much in doubt. In that case we
might even win, with a minnow achieving great things, and
"Viktorian" politics becoming globally influential, as it finds
resonances across the world.

American conservatives also see that Soros is well into his
nineties and is losing momentum. The old man may have
been a "philanthropist," but his son Alex cannot be, and
it is doubtful whether he will have the ability to manage
networks that his father had. If Donald Trump is elected
in November, if Israel emerges victorious from the conflict
with Hamas and Iran, and the Soros NGOs can be sidelined,
then the Soros network's light will slowly fade. While there
may be other networks (for example those of Bill Gates and
Bill Clinton, and other global foundations), people now are
more suspicious of America than they were in the 1990s.

So a breakthrough is needed. If this does not happen,
then Orbán's success will have been that he has bought us
time and another decade or two of normality. If the world
does not move, all we can do is poke, prod, and annoy,
getting on everyone else's nerves. As the Dalai Lama once
said: "If you think you're too small to make a difference,
try sleeping with a mosquito." But few of us would bet that
there will not be a Third Punic War at some point.

UNSPECIFIED YEAR

If there is a God...

The battle between Orbán and Soros is like the battle between *somewhere* and *anywhere*. There is nothing wrong with being anywhere if in the meantime you can be somewhere; but Soros's promise is about the domination of *anywhere*.

The world of anywhere can only win if it can find a generation whose members it can tear from the roots that we ourselves are. Because this whole fight is not just about migration, nations, or gender. It is about two opposing world forces, and whether we believe that there is an order that transcends us which we have no power to change, and in which origin, blood ties, and a collective sense of belonging are important motivating principles. Or do we say that there is no such order, that the only guiding principle is that you can be at home anywhere, and it does not matter to whom you belong, or to whom you are bound by ties and obligations? The Soros types do not care where they come from: they are not French, not Polish, not German. They can be at home anywhere, and have nowhere to go home to. This is a kind of childlike irresponsibility. Meanwhile, Orbán's struggle is wholly Christian: "Take up your cross, and do what you must! You have a community from which you cannot break away; you can go anywhere, but you will return, because you are *somewhere*. You belong here. Take up your cross, take on responsibility, and together we will build a successful nation!"

The conflict between the two world forces is irresolvable, and it is also a metaphysical or theological conflict.

According to Soros, the world we live in can be changed: we can change its foundations. There is no pre-ordained order that cannot be changed by human will and intention. It can be for good or for bad. What is good and what is evil is determined solely by us: by whoever is stronger, whoever has more money, whoever invents a better story about himself, whoever manages to portray himself as the embodiment of Good and his opponent as Evil. Soros is the philanthropist, the benefactor who wants good and wants to make the world a better place. Since Orbán goes against this, Orbán can only be evil and bad.

And from Orbán's point of view, those things which you have been taught are good and which you accomplish will be incorporated into the world that you leave behind. In fact you will not get your reward in heaven, but this itself will be your reward. And the punishment, the damnation, will be that if you were on the wrong side, after death everything you have done will be erased, destroyed with you — as if you had never existed, as if you had never been here, as if you had never been born. Orbán says he is on the road to salvation, while Soros is on the road to perdition. He is not simply falling into oblivion when sifted through the sieve of time. It is even worse than that, for when in the future there is again a war being fought for the cause of a good world, Soros will be cited as the demon who was on earth earlier and who must always be confronted. His name will forever be the name of damnation, and he will never be mentioned as being on the good side, always only on the bad side. And it will not be the soldiers of the bad who speak his name, but the soldiers of the good — just as the soldiers who fought in the Crusades said that the battle would always be fought against such demons.

And, of course, one can see Orbán and Soros as being like two popes. Each has his own virtue and his own original sin. What Orbán stands for has its appeal, and what Soros stands for also has its appeal, because it also comes from within you: that you want to be free, and do not want to accept the constraints imposed on you.

When the hated Cardinal Richelieu — that embodiment of intriguing evil — died of pleurisy in December 1642, the heavily taxed peasantry erupted in jubilation. During the French Revolution his tomb was even opened up and his corpse decapitated — as was the practice with traitors. Then it was thrown into the Seine. All that remained of it was the skull, which was eventually hidden by monks in the Sorbonne Chapel.

When Pope Urban VIII was informed of Cardinal Richelieu's death, he is reported to have said: "If there is a God, Cardinal Richelieu will have much to answer for. If not . . . well, then he had a successful life."

If there is no God, Orbán and Soros are just as right as each other. They both stand in the same position, and both will receive the same judgement; it is just that one wanted this and the other wanted that. So on what basis would we choose between the two?

But, if there is a God...

Epilogue

I AM SITTING IN A CINEMA WATCHING Ridley Scott's film about Napoleon. Somewhere in the middle of the film, Napoleon says, "I am certain I will bring the laurels of another glorious victory to my army today." Just then my phone vibrates.

It is Orbán.

I stand up and walk out of the cinema, call a cab, and in twenty minutes I am in Orbán's office in Buda's former Carmelite Monastery. Initially he shows slight resentment at having had to wait for me; as I was not there right away, he had decided to sleep a little (for about seven or eight minutes). Then he continues, "I hear you're writing a book about Soros. What I want to say is that, unlike the authors of pro-Soros books, who always describe Soros as a businessman and philanthropist of Hungarian origin, I don't consider him to be just of Hungarian origin, but a Hungarian. And I don't mean just in a formal, legal sense, but also in reality. If George Soros is ever in danger somewhere, he can certainly count on me, and on the Hungarian state. Because he's a Hungarian, a Hungarian citizen, and must be rescued if he's ever in danger. This is despite the fact that I also say that the Left is part of the nation like the 'ill fate' mentioned in "*Himnusz*" [the Hungarian national anthem]. So he is part of our nation, and that is horrific. But he is still part of our nation."

On my way out, I was continuously occupied with the thought that although there can be no compromise in the struggle between Orbán and Soros, a conflict that is irreconcilable, it seems after all that there is something in us that not only elevates their struggle but also elevates this something above their struggle.

For although Soros is implacable, he is convinced that political leaders come and go, but the university is eternal. So, he thinks, when all this is over and Orbán is no longer Prime Minister of Hungary, his university will return here and we will find out who or what is more lasting than bronze. Because until the day he dies Soros will certainly not accept that here he has been defeated. So there is still work to be done. And as long as there is unfinished work, there will be a fight. Yet shortly after thinking all this, I hear that Soros has supposedly made a will stipulating that when he leaves this world he should be laid to rest in Budapest's Farkasréti Cemetery.

I wonder to myself what it is that I am looking for, what it is that makes me uneasy, that makes this duel so elemental. And then, sure enough, it dawns on me! They are Hungarians. Or, to clarify, I see that this is how we Hungarians are: a people that has suffered much and that amazes the world. One is a Hungarian, the other is a Hungarian—or could have been... Anyway, only we Hungarians can be so interesting, because only we go into battle with this on our lips: "God, do not help us, simply marvel at this!"

ABOUT THE AUTHOR

GÁBOR G. FODOR graduated in Political Science from the Faculty of Humanities of the University of Miskolc in 1999. He received his PhD from the Institute of Political Science of the ELTE in 2003 and his habilitation in 2011. He taught for almost a decade and a half at the Institute of Political Science of ELTE, for three years at the Institute of Political Science of Corvinus University of Budapest, and for four years as a young research fellow at the Institute of Political Science of the Hungarian Academy of Sciences. He has held several research fellowships in Austria (2000, 2003, 2007), was a visiting lecturer at Aoyama Gakuin University in Tokyo (2010), and has been a fellow of the 21st Century Institute (2000–2001, 2003–2004). In 2005 he won the Academy Youth Prize; in 2007 he was awarded the Aurel Kolnai Prize for the best political science publication of the year; in 2008 he was awarded the Bezerédj Prize; and in 2009 he received the MTA Bolyai Plaque for outstanding research. Since 2021 he has been the Strategic Director of the 21st Century Institute. He has written books on bourgeois radicals and Eric Voegelin's political philosophy and governance, among others. His books published by the Foundation for Research in Central and Eastern European History and Society include *The Orbán Rule* (2021); *Political Virology—Governing the Virus* (2021); *The Man with the Knife—A Thought War* (2023); and the present work, *Orbán vs. Soros* (2024).